The Participatory Creativity Guide for Educators

The Participatory Creativity Guide for Educators debunks our out-dated cultural understanding that some people are creative and others are not. Offering an embracing approach to creativity that encompasses invention and innovation, this practical guide reframes creativity as a mode of experience that all young people and adults have the opportunity to participate in.

Bringing the principles of participatory creativity into the classroom, this book helps educators reframe invention and innovation, democratize the creative process, and leverage the knowledge, skills, background experiences, and cultural per-spectives that students bring with them every day. Key concepts are illustrated through rich vignettes and pictures of practice as chapters walk you through the what, why, and how of incorpo-rating participatory creativity into your teaching and learning environment.

Designed for educators in a vast array of settings (including schools, community centers, museums, afterschool programs, and grandpa's backyard workshop), this book is key reading for any educator looking to use creativity to strengthen and expand their teaching and learning.

Edward P. Clapp is a principal investigator at Project Zero and a lecturer on education at the Harvard Graduate School of Education in Cambridge, Massachusetts.

Julie Rains is a longtime educator and the current instructional innovation program consultant for Rochester Community Schools in Rochester, Michigan. Julie facilitates a variety of in-person and online professional learning experiences through her work with Project Zero at the Harvard Graduate School of Education.

T0383691

Other Eye on Education Books
Available from Routledge
(www.routledge.com/eyeoneducation)

Teaching Signature Thinking
Strategies for Unleashing Creativity in the Classroom
John Lando Carter and Kevin S. Krahenbuhl

Your First Year
How to Survive and Thrive as a New Teacher,
Second Edition
Todd Whitaker, Madeline Whitaker Good, and Katherine
Whitaker

The Student Motivation Handbook
50 Ways to Boost an Intrinsic Desire to Learn
Larry Ferlazzo

Visualize Your Teaching
Understand Your Style and Increase Your Impact
Kyle Ezell

Specially Designed Instruction
Increasing Success for Students with Disabilities
Anne M. Beninghof

Teach from Your Best Self
A Teacher's Guide to Thriving in the Classroom
Jay Schroder

The Participatory Creativity Guide for Educators

Edward P. Clapp and Julie Rains

Routledge
Taylor & Francis Group

NEW YORK AND LONDON

Designed cover image: Julie Rains

First published 2024
by Routledge
605 Third Avenue, New York, NY 10158

and by Routledge
4 Park Square, Milton Park, Abingdon, Oxon, OX14 4RN

Routledge is an imprint of the Taylor & Francis Group, an informa business

ISBN: 978-0-367-68327-6 (hbk)
ISBN: 978-0-367-67827-2 (pbk)
ISBN: 978-1-003-13695-8 (ebk)

DOI: 10.4324/9781003136958

Typeset in Palatino
by SPi Technologies India Pvt Ltd (Straive)

Contents

Illustrations

Figures

Table

Meet the Authors

Edward P. Clapp, Ed.D. is a principal investigator at Project Zero—a research center at the Harvard Graduate School of Education in Cambridge, Massachusetts—interested in exploring creativity and innovation, design- and maker-centered learning, contemporary approaches to arts teaching and learning, and diversity, equity, and inclusion in education. Edward lives on the Northshore of Massachusetts, where he enjoys futzing around with any number of half-complete home improvement projects, attempting to grow vegetables, trying to figure out how to sail, painting in his garage, or enjoying the beach—year-round, rain (snow!) or shine—with his wife and two young children.

Julie Rains, Ed.S. is an Instructional Innovation Program Consultant at the Rochester Community Schools, a public school district in Rochester Hills, a suburb of Detroit, Michigan. Over the past 15 years, she has had the opportunity to work with a diverse range of students in grades K-12 (as well as adult learners) and has experience in a wide range of educational disciplines. Julie is committed to continually improving the field of education as a faculty member at the Project Zero Classroom Summer Institute at the Harvard Graduate School of Education, Project Zero online coach and instructor, and instructional designer. A maker at heart, she is always looking for the next object to transform into something new, which comes in especially handy as she and her husband try to keep their twin boys busy around their old farmhouse.

Acknowledgments

At the heart of the concept of participatory creativity are the importance and value of socially distributed idea development. To that end, we would like to thank and acknowledge the many stakeholders who have come together to support the development of the tools, strategies, and ideas in this book.

Paramount among those individuals is Michael Hanchett Hanson, one of the primary originators of the concept of participatory creativity. Michael is an active and cherished mentor—and a lodestar for advocating for more distributed and participatory approaches to invention and innovation. We are grateful for his contributions to this work.

We likewise owe our gratitude to all of the practitioners who have been such an important part of this idea development process, including Sharonne Blum, Vidya Ganesh, Dolph Hardigree, Lee Howard, Jennifer Kain, Erik Lindemann, Matt Littell, Erika Lusky, Rachel Mainero, Jere Lorenzen-Strait, Ilse Ortega, Joyce Pereira, Jodie Ricci, Yerko Sepúlveda, Justine Smith, and Kym Strozier.

We are especially thankful for the young innovators (and their parents!) who have contributed to this work, including Charlotte Own and Girls of the Crescent—Mena and Zena Nasiri.

We would like to further express our appreciation to our good friends and colleagues Jeff Evancho and Peter Wardrip for sharing their thoughts on documentation and assessment in a rich and meaningful way.

A number of schools and organizations played a key role in formally supporting professional development initiatives and other activities that contributed to the tools, strategies, and ideas expressed in this book. Among these schools and organizations are Bialik College in Melbourne, Australia; Whole Mind Design in Ann Arbor, Michigan; and Rochester Community Schools in Rochester, Michigan.

We would like to additionally extend our gratitude to our many peers and colleagues at Project Zero, most especially Shari Tishman, Daniel Wilson, Sarah Sheya, and Faith Harvey.

As with many theory-to-practice projects, this book would not have been possible without the explicit and implicit support of our many thought partners in the world, including Mark Church, Janine de Novais, Vlad Glăveanu, Diana Lockwood-Bordaña, Cameron Patterson, Jim Reese, Ron Ritchhart, Jessica Ross, and S. Lynneth Solis.

We are further grateful for the persistent patience and support of our editors—Alexis O'Brien, Nicole Salazar, and Misha Kydd—and for the help of their team at Routledge.

As anyone who has written a book or undertaken a similar project will know, developing a manuscript is not a 9 to 5 job that you leave at the office. In this regard, we owe our deepest gratitude to the friends and family members, who have held us up (and bore with us!) as we worked to complete this project.

Julie would like to thank Jean Bolinger, Jennifer Conway, Michelle Dauzy, Katie Aramian, and Emma Okeson, her best friends now and always. All of her students, both past and present, for teaching her the power of student voice and meaningful collective participation. Jeff Frankowiak, Cindy Lindner, and Robert Phelps for their unwavering support, mentorship, and encouragement. She would also like to thank Samantha Marr at Rochester Community Schools and Paul Kennedy. Julie additionally expresses her gratitude to Ron Ritchhart for his guidance, mentorship, and introduction to the Project Zero world. Erika Lusky, the Statler to her Waldorf, official educational partner in crime, and the best friend anyone could ever ask for—this book would not have been possible without her. Her parents Ron and Pat Johnson and sister Amy for their unconditional love, support, and sacrifice to make her dreams a reality (and also for her recently discovered nickname, "The Princess"). Her little men and joyful distractions Carter and Riley Rains for all of the extra hugs and spilling her many cups of coffee while writing this book and, of course, her amazing husband Tyler for his unconditional love, support, and encouragement, especially through such an epically challenging year. Finally, Julie would like to dedicate this book to Christian Brown: "I made a promise a long time ago that I would try to make a difference in the world to change things, and this is my attempt to keep that promise Mr. Brown."

Edward would like to thank Bob Kaufman, Metta McGarvey, Alisa Stein, his parents MaryJane and Ed Clapp, his father- and mother-in-law Anthony and Marueen Mittiga, his brother Chris Clapp, and his brother-in-law Matt Mittiga for the strength they have offered throughout the writing of this book—especially as it came together during such turbulent times. Above all else, Edward would like to express his extreme gratitude to his wife Angela Mittiga and his children Penelope and Edward Wolife for all of the love and joy they have brought to him throughout the writing of this book.

Lastly, Edward would like to express his extreme gratitude to his participatory partner in crime—and his great friend—Julie. Although, when she first heard this work, Julie realized that she could no longer consider herself a creative "person" (and was upset with him), she would like to extend her sincere appreciation to Edward for amplifying her voice and including her in this meaningful movement.

1

Introduction

The sun is starting to set on a brisk fall day in the downtown district of a city in the Northeast United States. Within an old townhouse repurposed as the workshop space for an afterschool program for public high school students, a group of teenagers from various neighborhoods are musing on the summer. As part of the program they participate in, the students have been challenged to develop creative ideas that address a particular scientific theme. One group of students is working together to develop a pair of solar-powered rollerblades. "Why not use the power of the sun when it's hot outside," one student suggests, "so you don't have to work up a sweat when you go rollerblading?" It's a good idea, and each student sets to tackling a different aspect of the challenge. Some look into the solar technology they'll need, others consider the design of the rollerblades, while still others begin to develop a marketing and publicity campaign. One of the students is Maria, a recent immigrant to the United States from a Spanish-speaking Caribbean country. Maria has never thought of herself as a creative individual, but through this project she has been able to apply her unique knowledge of life in a warm and sun-ripe island by suggesting how the sun has been a help and a hindrance in the land where she is from—and she's increased her proficiency in English along the way. Despite Maria's efforts and the work of her peers, ultimately the solar-powered rollerblades never come to be. But through the process of trying to make them happen, each kid involved in the project comes to understand not whether they are creative but how they can uniquely participate in creativity.

* * *

DOI: 10.4324/9781003136958-1

On the opposite side of the world in a day school in Melbourne, Australia, a middle-years student named Xavier struggles to find a role for himself in an upcoming student-written and -directed play about a topic he and his classmates are studying in science. Xavier is a student with an expressive language disorder who freezes up on stage, often forgets his lines, and doesn't feel he would be much help as a member of the band. But instead of focusing on deficits, Xavier focuses on his strengths. For example, Xavier knows that his analytical mind is excellent at organizing things. And so, while his peers are assigned acting roles and begin to rehearse their parts, Xavier starts to tend to the technical aspects of the performance. Before long, Xavier has made a role for himself as the stage manager—running the show from behind the scenes. Xavier may not identify as a creative kid—and his teachers might not identify him as such, either—but through his determination and the support of others, Xavier has found his very own on-ramp to participate in the creative process.

* * *

Back in the United States, in the warmth of a suburban media center in a public elementary school, a small group of students sifts frantically through brightly colored bits of paper. They have only ten minutes left to finish a football-themed creation, and finding just the right materials for their vision of the field goal posts is taking longer than expected. Working under pressure—and feeling a little frustrated by the process— a second-grade student named Brooklyn remarks, "I told you, I'm just not creative." A chorus of student voices refute Brooklyn's self-doubt. Nonetheless, Brooklyn decides she needs a break from the action—as more hands begin searching for the elusive materials they need for the goal posts. Several minutes of group work go by while Brooklyn sits on the sidelines. Then a voice rings out, "How about these?" It's Brooklyn. Smiling triumphantly, she delivers a handful of materials to her group. The materials that Brooklyn has found are different from the ones the team was looking for—but they'll do the job—perhaps even better than what the group had in mind. With the new materials in hand, Brooklyn and her peers finish the piece just as the timer buzzes. While Brooklyn may have had misgivings, her classmates' actions and encouragement demonstrate the socially distributed nature of creative work—and the power of community participation in the development of students' creative identities.

What the above vignettes describe are not instances of creative genius exhibited by gifted and talented young people but rather examples of creative ideas and processes taking shape in a manner that provides multiple ways for a variety of young people to participate in invention and innovation. This brand of socially distributed idea development is known as participatory creativity. Early described by Edward P. Clapp in the 2016 Routledge text, *Participatory Creativity: Introducing Access and Equity to the Creative Classroom*, participatory creativity suggests a reframing of invention and innovation that is meant to democratize the creative process by leveraging the knowledge, skills, background experiences, and cultural perspectives that young people bring

FIGURE 1.1 When young people work together to develop a creative idea, they each have the potential to participate in creativity in their own unique way.

Illustration by Julie Rains.

with them to school (and various other teaching and learning environments) each day.

What Is Participatory Creativity?

If you live in the West or Global North, maybe you have had this experience: you walk into a school or classroom and your eye catches the image of Albert Einstein or Pablo Picasso or Steve Jobs or some other eminent innovator on a poster that is tacked to the wall. More often than not, the icon emblazoned in ink is a white male—probably a long-deceased white male. Below the image of this individual is a pithy quote or an aspirational phrase meant to inspire creativity. Whatever the text, the message the poster conveys is the same: *work hard and you can be like this guy one day.*

While the purpose of posters like these is meant to be inspiring, they may actually have alienating effects. For starters, most kids don't even look like the image of the icons on these posters. So immediately, there is a dissociation between the celebrated figure and the student staring up at them. But more importantly, the narrative surrounding the figure is likely to be one of extraordinary genius. Sure, these inspirational posters may motivate some students, but it is also possible that a discussion of such posters among students will go something like this:

Student 1: Didn't Einstein have some sort of superhuman brain that made him smarter than anyone else in the universe?
Student 2: Isn't his brain still in a jar somewhere, being studied by scientists to figure out what made him so genius-tastic?
Student 1: I'm pretty sure I don't have a superhuman brain that is genius-tastic… so how can I possibly be like that guy one day?

OK. We understand that we are getting a bit reductive and silly here. And, of course, we understand that not all inspirational creativity posters feature the likenesses of such men. There are also such posters depicting women and people of color from many different racial and cultural heritages (and, yeah, there are also inspirational creativity posters featuring images of rainbows or unicorns or the sun setting on the ocean, but we're not going there). Regardless of the icon or the image, the paradigm for creativity in which these posters are set is the same: a traditional individualistic approach to creativity that promotes a greater-than-thou narrative, situating creative people as those who are in some way more talented and gifted than the rest of us—regardless of what the inspirational text may say.

Participatory creativity takes this narrative and turns it on its head. From the perspective of participatory creativity, creativity is not something a single gifted individual *is* or *has*; rather, it is a process that all people can *participate* in. Participation, here, is understood as making a contribution to a broader idea from one's own unique social and cultural perspective. Reframing creativity in this way is meant to take a more democratic approach to invention and innovation that invites all people in. Later in this book, we'll explore the core principles of participatory creativity, but in order to address definitions upfront, we offer this:

> Participatory creativity is the process of engaging a distributed network of individuals in the development of creative ideas. Young people and adults play a variety of roles when they participate in creativity, each leveraging their own talents, skills, background experiences, and cultural perspectives.

Phew… that was a mouthful! We'll unpack this definition (and add to it a bit) a little later on, but for now, we hope that this reframing of creativity inspires you to consider how all young people in your classroom, in your afterschool program, in your community group, or in your family may find a means to realize their creative potential by uniquely participating in the development of creative ideas (see Figure 1.2). As we address this big topic, we'll also talk a bit about some elemental concepts like the important role that *roles* play in participatory creativity, the *socially distributed* nature of invention and innovation, how we can support students by making their *profiles of participation* visible, and a cool thing called *the biography of an idea*.

FIGURE 1.2 Young people and adults play a variety of roles when they participate in creativity, each leveraging their own talents, skills, background experiences, and cultural perspectives.

Illustration by Julie Rains.

And while we explore all of this, we'll address some time-honored questions: *How is this different from group work? Aren't you just describing project-based learning? All this sounds good for extroverted students, but what about the introverts in my classroom?* And, of course, our favorites: *But what about the students in my classroom who create amazing work all by themselves?* and *How do you assess all of this stuff?*

The *What, Why,* and *How* of Participatory Creativity

Since the publication of *Participatory Creativity* several years ago, educators from around the globe have developed strategies for incorporating the theory into practice. While a handful of examples of participatory creativity exist and there are a smattering of tools and practices floating about in the world, there is no one resource for practitioners interested in applying the principles of participatory creativity into their teaching and learning environments. And that's where this book comes in.

To make this book most useful for practitioners, we have taken a *what, why*, and *how* approach. In other words, our goal is for you to understand *what* participatory creativity is, *why* it is important, and—most importantly—*how* this practice has been enacted in a variety of classrooms and how you might incorporate this work into your own teaching and learning environment—wherever that may be. In particular, you will find that we present the what and the why of participatory creativity in Chapters 2, 3, and 6 and the how of participatory creativity in Chapters 4 and 5.

Participatory Creativity in Practice

Beyond tools and big ideas, we believe it is important to share stories of participatory creativity in action. That's why you will find many different *pictures of practice*—or case studies—throughout this book that provide windows into the work of practitioners applying the principles of participatory creativity in a variety of teaching and learning environments. In the chapters ahead, you will meet Joyce, a Brazilian-American educator working in Seoul, Korea as a computer science teacher who supports her students in identifying the human needs behind the apps, algorithms, and gadgets we use today, to identify what might be the next app, algorithm, or gizmo that will shape our lives tomorrow. You will meet Yerko, a Chilean-American educator who teaches Spanish to students at a school in the suburbs of Cleveland, Ohio. Yerko uses artifacts as a means of tapping into individual student interests to learn language by drawing on the wisdom of their communities. You will also meet Miriam, an Australian educator who teaches art in the suburbs of Melbourne, in the state of Victoria, Australia. Miriam has developed strategies for inviting introverted students into the creative process by tapping into their unique strengths and interests. Along with Joyce, Yerko, and Miriam, a host of other educators will be introduced, each with their own take on incorporating the principles of participatory creativity into their practice.

Beyond professional educators, you will meet young people engaging in the practice of participatory creativity, including Charlotte, a middle school student in Washington state who has worked with an online community to teach herself and her virtual friends how to code—and how to build their own online *sandboxes* where they share their ideas with one another and explore their interests. You will also meet Mena and Zena, two sisters in the suburbs of Detroit who have leveraged the power of their community to establish a not-for-profit organization called *Girls of the Crescent*. The purpose of their organization is to bring more books featuring female Muslim characters into schools.

Some of the pictures of practice that you will encounter in this book will be fully fleshed-out narratives, whereas others may be vignettes. In each case, we have endeavored to make connections between the picture of practice being presented to implications for practice—including links to theory and, in many cases, concrete tools and strategies that you can use in your own teaching and learning environment.

You will meet many practitioners through the pictures of practice presented in the pages ahead. But first you will meet the authors.

Meet the Authors

While many, many stakeholders have come together to explicitly and implicitly contribute to the tools, strategies, and ideas expressed in this book, two people came together in the roles of co-authors to put pencil to paper (or, rather, to peck away at their keyboards) to write this book: Edward P. Clapp, Ed.D. and Julie Rains, Ed.S.

Edward is a Principal Investigator at Project Zero—a research center at the Harvard Graduate School of Education in Cambridge, Massachusetts—interested in exploring creativity and innovation, design and maker-centered learning, contemporary approaches to arts teaching and learning, and diversity, equity, and inclusion in education. Edward and his Project Zero colleagues explore these issues with their teacher partners through a variety of collaborative inquiries around the world. In addition to working as a researcher, Edward is a Lecturer on Education at the Harvard Graduate School of Education. When he is not traveling around the world to work with educators, you can find Edward on most days at his home on the Northshore of Massachusetts, where he enjoys futzing around with any number of half-complete home improvement projects, attempting to grow vegetables, trying to figure out how to sail, painting in his garage, or enjoying the beach—year-round, rain (snow!) or shine—with his wife and two young children.

Julie is an Instructional Innovation Program Consultant at the Rochester Community Schools, a public school district in Rochester Hills, a suburb of Detroit, Michigan. Over the past 15 years she has had the opportunity to work with a diverse range of students in grades K-12 (as well as adult learners) and has experience in a wide range of educational disciplines. Julie holds degrees in elementary education, Language Arts, and Special Education (in the areas of Learning Disabilities and Emotional Impairments) as well as an educational specialist degree in Leadership and her administrator certificate. She is currently working on her dissertation examining the impacts of maker-centered learning as a special education intervention. A former Instructional technology consultant, information literacy specialist, and special educator, Julie is passionate about convincing all of you students and educators out there that you have valuable things to contribute to creativity, the arts, innovation, and leadership by remixing hands-on making opportunities with cutting-edge digital tools. She finds true joy co-designing alongside students to create unique and innovative learning adventures. Teaching is not only her profession, it is her passion. Julie is committed to continually improving the field of education as a faculty member at the Project Zero Classroom Summer Institute at the Harvard Graduate School of Education, as a Project Zero online coach and instructor, and as an instructional designer. Julie finds inspiration from her travels around the world and appreciates the beauty of small moments. A maker at heart, she is always looking for the next object to transform into something new, which comes in especially handy as she and her husband try to keep their twin boys busy around their old farmhouse.

Edward and Julie first met at a conference for educators in Atlanta, Georgia, where they were each presenting interactive workshops that supported creativity and innovation that focused on addressing issues of access, equity, and inclusion. During a social event at that conference, Edward and Julie—along with their colleague Erika Lusky—connected and have been good friends ever since.

In the years that followed their first connection, Edward and Julie began to see the need to develop a book about participatory creativity that was especially geared toward practitioners. With the support of many of the individuals represented in this book (and others!), Edward and Julie began to tinker with a handful of practitioner-based tools and strategies for supporting participatory creativity in a variety of settings. When Edward was approached by his publisher to write a second edition for the original *Participatory Creativity* book, he graciously declined the offer, suggesting to write this practitioners' guide instead. Given their experience working together and their shared passion for providing the tools, resources, and important pictures of practice they knew educators needed to support more socially distributed and participatory approaches to creativity in their classrooms, Edward and Julie decided to team up as co-authors. To this end, Edward brought his strengths as a scholar, theorist, and qualitative researcher (not to mention his penchant for wordplay and writing), while Julie brought her strength and experience as a classroom teacher, online instructor, maker educator, humanitarian, and master of all things whimsy (not to mention her talent as a sketch-note artist and her passion for graphically representing narratives and complex ideas). Together, Edward and Julie (that's us!) hope to have brought the best of themselves to this book—to best bring the concept of participatory creativity to life for you.

But wait—there's more…

In the initial *Participatory Creativity* book, Edward felt the importance of stating his positionality—in other words, acknowledging who he was and making his identity known to his readers. He did this for many reasons. Two such reasons were that Edward noticed a glaring lack of positionality in creative studies texts—and, to some degree, in practitioner-based educational texts as well. He found this to be problematic because not stating one's positionality suggests either that the identity of the author doesn't have bearing on the information being shared or that a normative perspective (likely white and male) is to be expected from academic and practitioner-based literature—or both. Neither of those things is good. Additionally, Edward had recently co-taught a course at the Harvard Graduate School of Education, where his students had called out him and his co-instructor for designing a syllabus that largely lacked author positionality. The students were right in raising this issue, and Edward and his co-instructor changed their approach to practice by including a new set of "critical lenses" on the course texts to probe perspective (we'll talk more about these critical lenses in Chapter 3).

Rather than present an objective "view from nowhere" that suggests that creativity research, theory, and pedagogical practice are socially and culturally neutral,[1] we believe that—just like anything else—creativity research, theory, and pedagogical practice are socially and culturally charged (this is a point expressed in the initial *Participatory Creativity* book).[2] This being the case, in the pictures of practice that we present in Chapter 4, we have asked our colleagues to briefly share a bit about their identities so that you, the reader, can have a sense of who they are and where they are coming from. At the same time, we, as authors of this text, feel it is important for us not only to share the bio statements we have presented above but also to state our positionality, so you, the reader, can know a bit more about who we are as authors and where our perspectives are coming from. So here goes: Edward and Julie are both white, cis-gendered (Edward's a man, Julie's a woman), middle-/upper-middle-class, educated Americans of Western European descent. Edward was born and raised in the Northeast United States (he's from Long Island and a Mets fan!), and Julie was born and raised in the Midwest (she's a proud Michiganer!). Julie is also the proud mom to two neurodiverse children, a fact she believes has largely influenced her perspective as an educator and human being in general. Generationally speaking, Edward is squarely a Gen X-er child of the Seventies, whereas Julie may be best described as a millennial. We hope that by knowing our positionality, you'll have a clearer sense of our perspectives as individuals in the world as you engage with the ideas and information that we present in the chapters to come.

A Bit about Process and Context

Although this book was published in 2024, we began working on it just before the COVID-19 global pandemic kicked in. Maybe you are like some of the folks we have all heard about on the news—or during virtual staff meetings—who suddenly had so much free time on their hands, they decided to teach themselves to play piano or to take online cooking classes to master the art of French cuisine or to finally write that novel or to develop a workout regimen that would frighten elite-class triathletes—or to develop an intimate relationship with something called a "sourdough starter." We think that is great! But we are not those people.

For myriad reasons, we found it difficult to find the time, attention, and clarity of mind to write a book during the COVID years. We're not looking for pity here, we're just being transparent about the fact that the COVID-19 pandemic was hard for us and it affected this project. We're sure that the pandemic was hard for many of you, too, and that so many of you have a story of struggle to share that equals or exceeds our own.

This being the case, we're ever grateful to our publisher Routledge for sticking with us as we consistently extended the deadline for this manuscript. Our editors have had the patience and forgiveness of the most tolerant Buddhists and saints. Thank you, all.

Here, we find it important for the reader to know that many of the interviews that we conducted for this book took place either pre-pandemic or during the early days of the pandemic. We've done our best to keep the ideas in this book—and most of all the pictures of practice we present in Chapter 4—fresh and alive. Given that the recent pandemic coincided with a brief moment in history that was dubbed "the big quit" and "the great resignation," many of the folks that we highlight throughout this book have moved onto their own next chapters since we connected with them. Wherever possible, we've included a "where are they now" note both to be transparent about the time that has passed since our colleagues first shared their stories with us and to celebrate how these intrepid educators, administrators, and students have grown and developed in their work and practice.

Another important note about who you will hear from in the pages ahead has to do with where we got our information. While the pictures of practice and tools offered in this book draw on educators from multiple countries spread across multiple hemispheres of the globe, you will note that there are three centers of gravity for this work. The first center of gravity is Rochester, Michigan in the United States, a distant suburb of Detroit in the southeastern part of the state. We're grateful for the uptake in participatory creativity that has happened among so many of our colleagues there. Another center of gravity for this work is Southwestern Pennsylvania in the United States. Within close proximity of Pittsburgh, Pennsylvania, our good friend Jeff Evancho has led the charge in supporting participatory creativity in this industrious part of the world. A third center of gravity is half a world away in the suburbs of Melbourne, Australia. Here, the good folks at Bialik College have been leaders in experimenting with participatory creativity through the Establishing Communities of Curiosity and Creative Participation program. You will hear from many voices in this book, but you should expect to hear from voices from these three participatory creativity centers of gravity a bit more than most. And that's a good thing! They have so much to teach us.

Who Should Read This Book?

If we were to take a truly participatory approach toward articulating the target audiences for this book, we would say that this book is meant for everyone and that, as diverse as each person's background and perspectives may be, there is something to be found in this book for all. Indeed, we believe that. But we also understand that having a few focal audiences in mind is useful. While we still aim to be all-inclusive, the primary audience for this book, as the title suggests, is educators. Of course, who an educator is can be considered in broad strokes. Indeed, people who show up for work in schools (or online) each day to teach students are educators, but so too are the many folks who work in museums, libraries, community centers, church basements, and any other number of formal or informal settings where teaching and learning take place. If you identify as an educator in this way, we're excited to have your eyeballs on these pages and eager to learn along with you and your students!

Beyond our primary educator audience, we see this book as being pertinent to an audience that consists of parents, school administrators, policymakers, and funders. Essentially, the way we think about this secondary audience is in terms of people who deeply care about teaching and learning and make decisions about what gets taught—and how it gets taught—in any variety of settings. This may include the members of the local parent–teacher association (PTA), the district superintendent, or the program staff at a foundation that supports education. We feel that people in these positions play pivotal roles not only in deciding what and how students learn but also in considering important issues pertaining to the future readiness of young people—as well as in determining how to make the spaces where creative learning experiences happen as accessible and as equitable as possible. Welcome to the conversation!

Not to put our good friends in academia at the end of the list, but a further audience for this book may include researchers interested in the study of creativity, invention and innovation, participation and participatory culture, systems thinking, issues of access and equity, or any number of other topics related to the fields of education or the creative sciences. While we are admittedly not going for deep scholarship here, we extend a warm welcome to our friends in academia, too!

How to Use This Book

Like many books, this educators' guide to participatory creativity can be read from front to back, from cover to cover, in a linear manner. Indeed, it was laid out in such a way that one chapter would support the information presented in the next. That being said, this book was also designed so that the busy educator might grab tools from one section of the book and refer back to key concepts or other contextual material later. This book was also designed for educators who wanted to further understand what the concept of participatory creativity might look like in action. For these educators, it may be helpful to read the pictures of practice presented in this book first and then to refer back to some of the tools or contextual chapters later.

However you choose to use this book. We encourage you to do three things: first, to pick this book up time and again, revisit chapters you've read previously, return to pictures of practice you've read before with fresh eyes, and to try and retry the tools and strategies in new ways. Second, we hope that you use the tools, strategies, and ideas presented in this book as a springboard to action in your classroom, your school, or your community. Dig in and try out a new practice. Third, share the love! If there is a concept, tool, or strategy that particularly resonates with you, we encourage you to share it with others at the coffee shop, at the next staff meeting, at the next PTA meeting, tomorrow morning at the bus stop, or at the next school board meeting. In much the same way, we encourage you to share any documentation from your classrooms, or insights and puzzles from your reading, with the broader educational sphere on social media. We'll be paying attention—and happy to be a part of the conversation @edwardpclapp @jj_rains #participatorycreativity.

A Road Map to the Journey Ahead

The structure of this book is meant to be a straightforward one that gradually builds from theory to practice. After this introductory chapter, we begin, in Chapter 2, with a practitioner-friendly crash course on the theory that undergirds participatory creativity. Rather than get deep into the academic weeds, we offer a rationale for participatory creativity at this moment in time and place an emphasis on the four key concepts that are foundational to a participatory reframing of invention and innovation: socially distributed idea development, biography of an idea, importance of role, and profiles of participation. This chapter will further make clear that issues of access, equity, and inclusion—though not discussed as a separate suite of concepts—are part of the DNA of participatory creativity.

In Chapter 3, we offer suggestions for how one might go about establishing a participatory creativity classroom. That chapter will serve as a practical guide for establishing a participatory creativity learning environment, including flexible structures that are meant to be applicable to educators in various settings.

The goal of Chapter 4 of this book is to make the work of participatory creativity visible through a host of case studies or *pictures of practice*. Set in a diverse array of teaching and learning environments throughout the United States and abroad, each of the pictures of practice offered in this chapter foregrounds one or more of the four key concepts described in Chapter 2 while applying a variety of the participatory creativity practices described in Chapter 3. Many of these pictures of practice also demonstrate one or more of the tools and strategies described in the participatory creativity tool kit offered in Chapter 5.

While stories are great, many educators need quick and easy access to tools that they can use. In Chapter 5, we offer just that, a tool kit for participatory creativity. That chapter functions as a self-serve reference bar where you can find pedagogical tools and strategies for incorporating participatory creativity into your practice. Designed to be actionable, user-friendly, and flexible, each of the tools presented in this chapter likewise includes recommendations for practice.

Lastly, in Chapter 6, we reflect on the five preceding chapters, consider further implications for practice, and offer a provocation or two to prod the work forward—and consider the future potential of the creative classroom. Way at the end of this book, you will find a complete bibliography, chock-full of the many sources that we have drawn upon in our writing—which you may be interested in further exploring to deepen your knowledge.

We have tried to keep the flow of this book as smooth as pudding, but at the same time we wanted to offer our readers as many resources and follow-up materials as possible. To that end you will occasionally notice superscripts in text as you read along. These refer to the notes at the end of each chapter. Here you will find additional commentary, resources, and other information to support your learning.

Putting together this *Participatory Creativity Guide for Educators* has been an exciting, insightful, and—above all—participatory experience for us. However you engage with the tools, strategies, and ideas in the pages ahead, we hope that you experience the same degree of excitement, insight, and spirit of participation that we did while writing this book.

Notes

1 See Nagel, T. (1986). *The view from nowhere*. New York: Oxford University Press.

2 See also Clapp, E. P. (2019). Introducing new voices to the creativity studies conversation: W. E. B. Du Bois, double-consciousness, and *The Souls of Black Folk*. In V. P. Glăveanu (Ed.), *The creativity reader* (pp. 543–559). New York: Oxford University Press.

2

Participatory Creativity 101

Maybe you've seen this before: a group of kids are given a design challenge, or an art project, or even a basic research project to work on together. The kids are slow to start the work, and honestly, if you look closely at who is in the group, you're not sure how these students complement one another—you're not even sure if they like one another. The project has a "creative" outcome associated with it. Once they get over their social awkwardness, one of the students just starts spurting out ideas, "Maybe we can do this, or this, or this, or this…." Another student is doodling in her notebook, while another student futzes around on social media, and yet another student just pretends to listen while bopping his head along to the music playing through his headphones. There doesn't seem to be cohesion in the group or even common purpose. The teacher stops by to see how things are going. Only the student with all of the big ideas speaks. She uses the "we" voice to say, "we might do this, or do this, or do this." The teacher is impressed. "Those are such creative ideas," she says to the ideating student and then asks the ideating student to share more. The ideating student expands upon one or two ideas, and the teacher responds, commends her for her work, and encourages her to push forward with her teammates. The teacher then turns to the others and says, "Guys— pay attention. So-and-So has some really exciting ideas for you to think about." The teacher then makes a series of quick and familiar hand gestures which are taken together to mean

DOI: 10.4324/9781003136958-2

stop-doodling-get-off-the-Internet-and-take-off-those-headphones. She then moves onto the next group of students—as the doodler, social media surfer, and headphone bopper roll their eyes.

This scene is familiar to all of the characters involved. Most notably, it is familiar to the doodler, social media surfer, and headphone bopper. They know that whenever they are asked to work in a group and be creative, what they have to contribute is rarely ever valued. They have come to understand and accept that in these situations, their teachers value students who can come up with big ideas. Other forms of creative participation are not valued—or even understood. Therefore, the doodler, social media surfer, and headphone bopper don't feel like they have anything to contribute to the creative process. But maybe there is another way to frame what creative *participation* looks like?

The Problem with Traditional, Individual-Based Understandings of Creativity

Here in the United States—and in many other countries around the world—popular understandings of what it means to be creative have long been associated with the celebration of works of invention that have pushed forward fields of practice: the first paintings and sculptures in a new art movement, groundbreaking scientific theorems, standout works of literature, rock albums that paved the way for wholly new genres of music, digital devices that have changed the way we work and play, medical breakthroughs, feats of engineering, social reforms, and social media platforms that have established themselves as new community spaces. Oftentimes, the inventions at the heart of an innovation are associated with the individuals who introduced them to the world. And it is true, such inventors deserve credit for the work they have done to move a domain of practice forward, but there is also risk involved in celebrating such individuals.

Because of the eminent status that they have achieved in their fields, these individuals are often held up as being creative *geniuses.* But if we were to peel back the layers of the contributions that each one of these individuals have made to science, the humanities, and culture, we will quickly see that—bright as any one creative producer may have appeared to be—the works that they are most known for were supported either directly or indirectly by the contributions of others. Nonetheless, the myth of the sole creative genius persists.

The form that the creative genius often takes in the classroom—as in the opening vignette for this chapter—is the *ideator* or the *divergent thinker*. Indeed, many "creativity tests" are not tests of creativity at all—they are tests of divergent thinking.[1] But ideation and divergent thinking are not the only ways to participate in creativity. Having a bias toward ideation and divergent thinking as being the markers of creativity certainly benefits the students who excel in those cognitive capacities—but it further alienates the many students who excel in other capacities.

The primary *why* of participatory creativity, then, is to provide an opportunity to make participation in creative learning experiences accessible to all students—regardless of where their social, cultural, or intellectual strengths lie.

In this chapter, we will provide a little bit of backstory on the sociocultural roots of participatory creativity before digging into the *what* of participatory creativity. In particular, we'll describe the four key concepts associated with participatory creativity before addressing some common pitfalls to look out for when adapting a participatory stance toward creativity in the classroom.

Moving toward a Sociocultural Understanding of Creativity

In the spirit of walking the talk, we feel it is important to recognize the roots of participatory creativity. As with any new theory or practice, the concept of participatory creativity draws upon concepts, theories, and practices that came before it. Most notably, the *sociocultural* reframings of creativity that developed in the 1980s and 1990s serve as springboards of this work.

During the tail end of the 20th Century, a handful of creativity scholars began to challenge the dominant narrative in creativity theory that honored the individual inventor. Instead, these scholars took a *systems-based* or *distributed* approach to describing the creative process.[2] Most notable among these scholars are Mihaly Csikszentmihalyi and Teresa Amabile. Early on, Csikszentmihalyi presented a systems theory that placed creativity at the center of individuals, domains, and fields. Around the same time, Amabile presented a social psychology–based theory that placed creativity in context. Contemporaneously, two Howards also contributed to more systems-based approaches to creativity: Howard Gardner and Howard Gruber. Gardner built on Cskiszentmihalyi's theory of individual, domain, and field, while Gruber proposed his own theory of networks of enterprise. As forward-thinking as the work of these scholars was, the individual creator still played a significant role in the theories proposed by each.

Not long after these scholars began to change the narrative around creativity theory, Keith Sawyer, a prolific creativity theorist, began to further propose reframings of creativity from the position of *social emergence, group genius, distributed creativity*, and *collaborative creativity*. In more recent times, the work of Michael Hanchett Hanson and Vlad Glăveanu (oh yeah, and Edward too!) further pushed our understanding of the social nature of creativity—each advocating for a more participatory approach to the phenomenon. The momentum toward asserting a sociocultural stance toward creativity has built up over the years—so much so that in 2019 a group of nearly two dozen scholars from around the world came together to write a sociocultural creativity manifesto.[3]

Establishing a more socially distributed understanding of creativity has by all means been a participatory process. Each successive wave of sociocultural creativity theory built upon the last, and many of the scholars developing this theory (including the few listed above and many others) have been close colleagues of one another, and many veteran scholars have served as mentors to emergent thinkers.

Beyond the narrative about the sociocultural roots of participatory creativity presented above, it is important to note that participatory creativity further draws on other theories and practices. A short list includes work related to distributed cognition, collective agency, systems theory, actor–network theory, and participatory culture.

There is lots to be said about the biography of the participatory creativity idea (don't get Edward started), but for the purposes of this *educators' guide*, we're going to leave it here. If you are interested in learning more about the theory and practice that informed this work, we encourage you to check out the References and Suggestions for Further Reading section of this book, review the original *Participatory Creativity* book, or read the entry on participatory creativity authored by Edward and his colleague Michaell Hanchett Hanson in the 2020 *Encyclopedia of Creativity*. You can also check out the Participatory Creativity Lab website, which includes lots of cool information and some really helpful case studies.[4]

What Makes Participatory Creativity Different from Other Brands of Sociocultural Creativity Theory?

OK. This is an easy one. The difference between participatory creativity and other sociocultural approaches to creativity is the emphasis it places on *participation*. What does participation mean? Let's try this out for starters:

> *Participation can be described as uniquely contributing to an activity or common purpose along with others.*[5]

That's a pretty straightforward definition that isn't a whole lot different from one you might find in an everyday dictionary—but there are nuances to it. In fact, there are three. We'll take them in order.

The first nuance is the word *uniquely*. When we participate in an activity or common purpose, we do not do so in the same way as everyone else. We do so in a way that is specific—or unique—to who we are. From this perspective, participation prompts individuals to bring aspects of themselves to a project or a broader purpose. In this way, it actively promotes diversity of thought, background, perspective, or experience. It also prompts people to bring their unique talents and skills to a project or a purpose. This connects to a concept that will be discussed more below: the important role that *roles* play within a participatory reframing of creativity. The idea of role leads to the concept of *contribution*.

The second nuance in the above definition of participation is the word *contributing*. When individuals participate in an activity or common purpose, they do so by contributing to its development in some way. Individuals contribute to the development of an activity or common purpose by playing unique roles.

The third nuance in the above definition is the back end of it: the two phrases that read *common purpose* and *along with others*. Even though these two phrases flow together in the definition above, it's helpful to discuss them separately. We'll take *along with others* first. When individuals participate in creativity, they inherently do so with others. One of the founding principles generated from the original *Participatory Creativity* book—and a common declaration made at many a participatory creativity professional development presentation—is that *no feat of invention or innovation occurs in isolation; creativity is always socially situated*. Therefore, at its heart, participation is not about engaging in an activity on one's own but rather about working with others to achieve a common objective. And that brings us to that other phrase we mentioned a few sentences ago: *common purpose*.

Quick history lesson: one of participatory creativity's forefathers was an American psychologist mentioned earlier named Howard Gruber. Gruber and his colleagues believed that all creative pursuits were intentional and wrote a good deal about *creativity as purposeful work*.[6] *Work* is a key word here. It means that creativity does not come without effort but rather requires committed energy. *Purpose*, of course, is also a key word; it means that the work of creativity is intentional, driven toward a particular objective, or, in other words, purposeful. And that all brings us back to participation as being about the act of *working with others to achieve a common purpose*. Phew!

So, What Makes Participatory Creativity *Creative*?

This is such a good question! It's also a messy one to answer—messy because it brings up a long-standing debate in the field of creativity studies over the issue of the letter c—or C—or a c/C that is a size somewhere in between.[7] What are we talking about? Some theorists hold to the idea of creativity from the perspective of big C. What is meant here is creative output of the variety that has the power to entirely change the course of a field of practice. You know the type—that scientific theory that changed the way we think about everything, that gadget that changed the way we do everything, or that hip-hop album that changed the way we hear and listen to everything. This is big C creativity, a reference to inventions and innovations that push beyond boundaries and reshape an aspect of our worlds. On the flip side of big C creativity is little c creativity. Little c creativity is often called everyday creativity. It's the artwork that kids bring home from school, a quick solution to a household problem (like using a wire hanger to fix a broken antenna), or a left-of-center sartorial choice that someone makes one day. Anytime you may have heard someone say "you're so creative" (i.e., if they really mean it, and they're not being snarky or passive aggressive), they are probably referring to little c, or everyday creativity.

Beyond the Big C and little c binary, there are those who advocate for mini c or middle C or those who see a spectrum of Cs between Big C and little c. From the perspective of participatory creativity, the size of c is no issue. Big C, middle C, little c, mini c, or any size of C in between—creativity is always socially and culturally distributed. The principles of participatory creativity apply no matter what the size of your C is.

This might all sound great, but the astute reader will note that we have still not answered the question in the heading for this section: *so what makes participatory creativity creative?* Two words provide us with an answer: *novelty* and *utility*. Novelty and utility won't be new concepts to most creativity theorists. In fact, they might be among the few things that most creativity theorists agree on. Creativity can be understood, in very broad terms, as the pursuit of novel ideas that are in some way useful

FIGURE 2.1 A community of people impacted by the development of a creative idea may be a whole field of practice, a globally distributed group of online participants, or a small group of friends in a classroom.

Illustration by Julie Rains.

to a community of people, however big or small. In this sense, a community of people may be an entire scientific field—or a small classroom—or a globally distributed group of online gamers—or just a few friends. So, to recap, what makes participatory creativity creative is the pursuit of novel ideas that are in some way useful to a community of people.

Why Reframe Creativity as a Distributed and Participatory Process?

The primary reason to reframe creativity as a distributed and a participatory process—especially within the field of education—is to democratize creativity, making creative learning experiences accessible to all young people and adults. It is an inclusive approach to creativity, one that intentionally invites the contributions of individuals from diverse backgrounds, each with their own talents, skills, background experiences, and cultural perspectives.

Traditional, individual-based understandings of creativity in education (and the psychometric tests that purport to measure individual student creativity) limit what engagement in the creative process may look like. It is these understandings that create the conditions where some learner contributions are valued more than others, sending messages that the doodler, social media surfer, and headphone bopper do not have something worthwhile to suggest or share in their group project. In contrast, participatory creativity throws the doors to creative participation wide open, creating the space for learners with diverse passions, interests, and perspectives to engage as equally valued contributors (see Figure 2.2).[8]

FIGURE 2.2 A participatory approach to creativity broadens our view of what creative engagement may look like—opening the doors for many people to participate in creativity in a variety of ways.

Illustration by Julie Rains.

In the original *Participatory Creativity* book, the need for a shift away from traditional, individual-based approaches to creativity, to a more participatory stance, was described in terms of the *eight barriers to access and equity in the creative classroom*. These eight barriers to creative participation were rooted in a set of five different *crises of creativity* stemming from a culture of individualism and three additional crises of creativity stemming from a culture of power. To further emphasize the *why* for participatory creativity, each of these crises of creativity is briefly described below.

Beyond presenting these multiple crises, we present possible solutions to overcome these crises. You'll note that these possible solutions are limited in scope, and you may see further solutions of your own to overcome these cultural barriers. We encourage that!

The Five Crises of Creativity Stemming from a Culture of Individualism

As discussed earlier, many traditional understandings of creativity stem from a culture of individualism which permeates Western culture, as it does in other parts of the world. When we say this, we intend not to undermine the power of the individual but rather to consider the messages being sent when the contributions of one individual are held in higher regard than the contributions of another.

Crisis 1: The "Some kids are more creative than others" misconception

Maintaining an individual-based stance toward creativity sets educators up to compare the creative abilities of one student with the creative abilities of another. If creativity is something one either *is* or *has*, then it makes sense that some students may be perceived as more or less creative than others. Taken a step further, an individual-based perspective of creativity may prompt educators to see young people and adults in a much starker light—determining that some young people and adults are creative and that others are not. The challenge in the creative classroom is to see beyond individual-based orientations toward creativity and to recognize that young people and adults are not more or less creative than one another but rather that they each have the potential to participate in creativity in their own unique ways.

Possible Solutions

Notice and name the "some kids are more creative than others" misconception for what it is—a misconception! Have a conversation with your students (in age-appropriate ways) about the falsity of some kids being more creative than others. Point out that no one is creative. And if no one is creative, then it's impossible for someone to be more creative than another. Instead, point out that creativity is a process and an experience in which all kids have the capacity to participate and that everyone in the room has a unique and important way to contribute to creativity. Take it a step further and engage your students in a conversation about their uniqueness—and how what makes them unique might bring value to a creative learning experience.

Crisis 2: The "I'm just not a creative person" syndrome

We've all heard it before from that student in our classroom, that colleague at work, or that family member: "I'm just not a creative person." It's the ultimate statement of creative defeat. *This creativity stuff is not for me—whatever is happening here, I don't belong here—I'm not even going to try.* That's a terrible way for young people and adults to engage in any sort of learning experience. And yet, messaging from schools and popular cultural may reinforce the idea that if young people and adults do not fit within a particular creativity mold, or if they do not excel on tests that are meant to measure creative ability, then it only makes sense that some young people and adults may just not see themselves as creative people. The challenge here is to push beyond the stereotypes associated with traditional understandings of creativity rooted in individualism and to take a stance that may be difficult for some to accept: *There is no such thing as a creative person.* Rather, there are multiple ways for all people to *participate* in creativity.

Possible Solutions
Acknowledge once again that there is no such thing as a creative person. Creativity is not something one can be or have; it is a process and an experience that everyone can participate in. Point out to your students how it does not make sense to worry about being a creative person or not, but it is very valuable to consider what types of people they actually are. Spend time with your students having an assets-based discussion about who they are and how their backgrounds, skill sets, and various aspects of their identity make them valuable to the work of creativity.

Crisis 3: Narrowly Defining Creativity Privileges Some Students and Alienates Others

Previously, we mentioned that oftentimes traditional, individual-based understandings of creativity narrowly focus on ideation and divergent thinking as markers of creative ability. And while ideation and divergent thinking may be helpful throughout the process of creative idea development, they are not the only cognitive capacities that are necessary to engage in invention and innovation. Whether it be ideation, divergent thinking, or some other suite of cognitive abilities, narrowly defining creativity naturally privileges some young people and adults who excel in those cognitive capacities while alienating other students who excel in other ways. Dispelling the idea that individuals are creative and impressing upon students that creative participation can take many forms are ways to provide on-ramps to creative learning experiences for young people and adults who may otherwise feel alienated from the work that takes place in the creative classroom.

Possible Solutions
Remind your students—and yourself—that there are multiple roles that young people may play when they participate in creativity. Have them consider the diversity of roles they play in creative work—or in any work, for that matter—when they are having the most fun and being their best selves. Emphasize that creative participation isn't just one thing, it's many things, and that each of your students has something to contribute to the development of creative ideas.

Crisis 4: Denying Young People the Opportunity to Create and Invent with Others

It's tempting to cite a vast and growing field of research that supports the idea that young people and adults invent and create more innovative solutions to problems—and learn more—when they work together as opposed to when they work by themselves. Research aside, many of you reading this book will intuitively know that kids and adults do their best—and most interesting—work when they engage with others. An individual-based orientation of creativity denies young people access to the important peer-to-peer, community-based, and contextually connected learning that takes place when students invent, solve problems, and build knowledge together. Understandably, some of you reading this book may say, *Hold on a second, there are students in my classroom and people I know who do their best work by themselves*. A response to this challenge may be: *Of course they do! Everyone needs time to work by themself once in a while*. An important point to make here is that a participatory approach to creativity is not a platform advocating for group work. When it suits young people and adults to work by themselves, they absolutely should. Here, a distinction needs to be drawn between *individual work* and *isolated work*. Individual work can still be connected to others—as opposed to being isolated from it.

Possible Solutions

Consistently provide opportunities for your students to work together on creative idea development projects. Disrupt traditional approaches to teaching and learning that situate students in rows at desks on their own; give them space to think and work together. Got an introvert in your classroom or someone who just works better on their own? Of course you do! We've all been that kid sometimes—and some of us just learn better that way. Nonetheless, as your loners are working away seemingly by themselves, ask them where their inspiration is coming from, help them make connections to the actions and ideas of others, and make the rich web of their thinking with all of its hidden social connections visible.

Crisis 5: Ill-equipping Young People for Success in Contemporary Life and Work

Perhaps the strongest case to be made for an emphasis on a participatory and distributed approach to creativity in education is the idea that our contemporary world—at its best—is not set up to support individual innovators working in isolation; the contemporary creative economy places much less of an emphasis on creative individuals working in isolation than it does on establishing interdisciplinary teams capable of approaching the process of innovation or creative problem-solving from multiple angles. An educational focus on individual creativity is incongruous with the needs of higher education settings and contemporary workplace environments. Therefore, the case can be made that educators who maintain an individual-based focus on creativity are ill equipping their students for success in life and work in the decades to come.

Possible Solutions

Take your students on field trips to local businesses—especially start-ups or other entrepreneurial settings. While they are there, have them notice and name the various roles that people play in that setting—maybe even interview them to learn more about what makes those individuals unique and what they specifically have to offer in the role at the company. Can't go on a field trip? Invite members from the community into your classroom to talk about who they are and what they do at work. Target your questions for your classroom guests around the unique roles they play in their workplace environment and ask them about who else they work with—either directly or indirectly—and how those people uniquely contribute to their work in different ways.

The Three Crises of Creativity Associated with a Culture of Power

While the five crises of creativity stemming from a culture of individualism are palpable, there are additional cultural forces that restrict access and engagement in the creative classroom—or in other creative idea development environments. Social and cultural structures, such as race and class, are at play within the creative classroom, just as they are at play within any classroom. Just like mathematics, literature, and social studies curricula—creative learning experiences don't just emerge from thin air—they come from someplace and therefore have an origin story. Just like any other curricular structure, creative learning experiences are not neutral; they are both socially and culturally charged.

In the original *Participatory Creativity* book, the challenges associated with the social and cultural origins of creative learning experiences were described in terms of the "three additional crises of creativity associated with our culture of power." Now some years later, we still feel these crises of creativity are important to consider, but we also feel that the language could use some refreshing. To start, the concept of *culture of power* is a reference to the work of Lisa Delpit, who, in some of her early writings about teaching and learning, addressed the role that power plays in the classroom.[9] We still believe this to be true, but we also believe that there are other structures in place (e.g., systemic racism and systemic poverty) that also limit access and equity in the creative classroom. In the original *Participatory Creativity* book, the word "our" was also used to describe the culture of power (and the culture of individualism). The problem here is that the word "our" suggests a definitive "us" who may be assumed to have a similar experience. To be more inclusive, it's best not to think in terms of "we," "our," and "us" but rather to think in terms of the broader concepts and structures—in this case, *a* culture of power—that each of us experiences differently. Lastly, in the original *Participatory Creativity* book, the three crises of creativity associated with a culture of power were described as being "additional" crises. This, too, needs revision, as the word "additional" suggests that the race and class-based structures described in this section are tacked-on experiences, which is inherently not true. Issues of inequity are central to the lived experiences of many people, as they are central to the experiences of many young people in a variety of teaching and learning environments. So, with some further thought, we're keeping some words and changing others as we consider the three crises of creativity associated with a culture of power.

Crisis 6: Assuming Creativity in Education Is Socially and Culturally Neutral

The field of creativity studies is changing all of the time. That being said, traditionally, white, Western men (or what some folks refer to as WEIRD men—people originating from Western, Educated, Industrialized, Rich, and Democratic cultures) made up the field of creativity studies—as they have made up the field of many other academic areas of practice.

Individual-based orientations toward creativity privilege certain *social and cultural profiles*. Because of the process of *social reproduction* and its presence in educational systems, students representative of the dominant culture of power may be more equipped to engage and/or excel in the creative classroom.[10]

Possible Solutions

Be curious and critical about the social and cultural origins of the curriculum you teach, and be candid with your students about where the content they engage with comes from. Don't shy away from potentially difficult conversations with kids about race, class, prejudice, and bias. Instead, go there. Go there on purpose. And go deep. As our good friend Janine de Novais once said, "if we talk to our children about race and racism in kindergarten, we won't have white fragility in college."[11] We firmly believe this to be true. At the same time, we further believe that a host of other social issues related to race, racism, prejudice, and bias would be ameliorated if we addressed those issues with our young people at an early age—just as Janine suggests—and then throughout their growth and development as they become older, wiser, and more sophisticated in their abilities to tackle such topics.

In addition to raising awareness, consider how you may bring a more diverse set of perspectives into the participatory creative classroom. Don't hesitate to bring parents, caregivers, and community members into the conversation about how to make the experience of invention and innovation more inclusive—and to support an overall sense of belonging for your students.

Remember, you've got lots of resources at your disposal. Access those resources and build on them to create the learning experiences that will most empower your students. Who your students are and what they have to offer come from where they come from. And where they come from is a rich and bountiful place!

Crisis 7: A Misalignment of Identity in the Representation of Creative Icons

The popular creativity narrative is prone to hold up certain individuals who have achieved eminence in their time as creative geniuses. Too often, these individuals are white men who do not look like the majority of students in schools and other creative learning environments today. Heralding larger-than-life individuals sends the message that achieving greatness is just for the gifted few, making creative achievement seem out of reach for many young people. An intentional and concerted effort to represent diverse cultural and social orientations toward creativity, coupled with a reduced emphasis on the achievement of the lone individual, can exemplify that there is a role for all learners in the creative classroom.

Possible Solutions

Flip the script and propose a counternarrative! First, acknowledge that the posters that your students see on the wall and that the individual-based narratives that kids hear about creativity are only half accurate and half true. Then, work with your students to investigate the biographies of the ideas that the creative icons they have been exposed to are known for. As you and your students investigate the biographies of these ideas, point out the diverse ways that various individuals have contributed to the development of these ideas over time. Whenever possible, make connections to the ideas you are exploring and your student population. Show how young people and adults just like them have played a role in the development of the creative ideas being heralded by the images and narratives that they are being exposed to. Most importantly, reinforce that your students have the potential to contribute to creative ideas in multiple ways, just like generations of people who look like them have done so in the past.

Crisis 8: An Imbalance of Opportunity

Cultures of power exist to perpetuate themselves. As a result, there is an imbalance of opportunity to participate in creative learning experiences that favors young people who have been raised in the culture of power. Children from wealthier families that have access to independent education or who live in more well-resourced school districts have more access to creative learning experiences than others. Too often, this inequitable access to creative learning experiences falls along the lines of race and class in the United States, as it does in other parts of the world.

Possible Solutions

It is very true that some children have more access to creative learning experiences than others. One way to address this inequity goes in the direction of awareness and activism—and we think those things are great. But we also think that a more immediate approach to addressing this crisis of creativity is to simply be the brave teacher who offers her students creative learning experiences regardless of who they are, what they look like, or how much their parents or caregivers make for a living—if they have parents or caregivers at all. In other words, just do it.

Earlier on, we suggested that one of the main goals of participatory creativity was to democratize creative learning experiences. We know that if you believe in the importance of engaging all young people in the process of invention and innovation as much as we do, then you can find a way to make it happen—for all students. You've picked up this book. You've found your way to these words in this chapter. You can do this.

Providing your students with the opportunity to engage in the process of creative idea development may be one of the most empowering things you can do for them no matter what you teach, where you teach, and whom you teach. Chapters 3, 4, and 5 will provide you with many resources to support you in this endeavor. But more important than what we have written in the chapters ahead is your personal conviction to provide your students with experiences that invite them into the creative process. If you are reading these words right now, we know you can do this.

The Four Key Concepts of Participatory Creativity

The concept of participatory creativity is rich and multilayered. It can seem like a lot to hold in one's head all at once—especially when faced with the fast pace and high demands of life as an educator! But the broader theory behind participatory creativity can be distilled down into four discrete concepts that are meant to be interrelated—with each concept supporting the others. Below, we lay out these four interrelated key concepts.

Socially Distributed Idea Development

Creativity is always socially and culturally situated.

At the heart of the theory of participatory creativity is the notion that no creative idea develops in isolation. Creativity is always socially and culturally situated. This may be a hard concept to grasp at first—especially if one has been raised within a culture of individualism, as is prevalent throughout most of the Western world. Nonetheless, if we were to probe the origin story of any creative idea, we would find that countless actors (human and otherwise) have contributed to the development of that idea over time.

"Over time" is important here. Contrary to the popular image of light bulbs used to symbolize creative insight, creative ideas never just materialize out of thin air. They bubble up slowly and have histories filled with the influences and contributions of many participants. Sometimes these influencers are easy to track, such as in academia where scholars cite their sources as they develop new theories. At other times, the socially distributed nature of idea development may be less easy to track, such as when an artist toiling away by herself inside a studio emerges years later with a genre-breaking painting style—or, more immediately, when you finally figure out the perfect quirky gift to get your spouse for your anniversary while you are taking your morning shower all by your lonesome.

Regarding the artist—sure, she may be working by herself in her studio as she develops her new style—but she is never actually *alone* in that space. Rather, all of her past influences are there

FIGURE 2.3 The four key concepts of participatory creativity.
Illustration by Julie Rains.

with her: every painting she has ever seen, every art class she has ever taken, every mentor, caregiver, heart break, you name it. All of those past experiences are there with her, and each of those experiences is influencing the artistic work she is developing as she is humming along to a Ben Webster or an xx album, mixing her paints, making marks, and making marks again.[12]

Regarding that flash of insight you may have had in the shower—the one when you finally figured out what to get your spouse for your upcoming anniversary—well… all your past experiences were in the shower with you, too! Many of us have had this sort of experience. We're in the shower, taking care of business, making sure everything is clean and where it is supposed to be, and then without putting thought into it, we figure something out, come up with a solution to a problem, or experience some other form of insight.

Why might this happen?

An armchair neuroscience explanation might be that when you overthink a problem, your neural network experiences a traffic jam of thought, and you can't figure out the solution to the problem you are trying to solve—or remember the name of that greasy spoon you and your friends used to haunt back in high school—because you are overthinking it. But when you are in the shower—y'know, taking a shower—your neural network frees up. You're focused on something else, using a different part of your brain, and then all of the sudden, the synapses start to fire and you figure out the problem you were puzzling over—and remember the name of the Starlight Diner.

This apparent moment of insight is beautifully described in French as *l'esprit de l'escalier* or "the spirit of the stairway."[13] A rough description of this phenomenon goes a little like this: You're at a party, deep into a conversation with your fellow revelers, who are each trying to outdo one another with their charm and wisdom. The conversation takes a curious turn toward the most creepy and campy music videos of the 1980s: "Sledge Hammer" by Peter Gabriel, "Land of Confusion" by Genesis, and "Rockit" by Herbie Hancock are all referenced. Laughter and cheers resound with each mention. But you've got the best one of all on the tip of your tongue, you can see it—the angel-winged goth kid throwing a dove, the flowing chiffon through blown open doors, the fencers, the greasers, the football players, the dancing ninjas, the water-drenched swim team, the choir boys with glowing eyes (they had glowing eyes!)—and all of that hairspray… but you just can't remember the name of that song.

Total cocktail conversation fail.

Then, hours later, after you've said your goodbyes and are blearily walking down the stairs on your way toward the door—while fumbling in your pocket for your car keys and trying to remember where you parked—it hits you: "Bonnie Tyler!" you shout aloud. "'Total Eclipse of the Heart!'" you shout again. The spirit of the stairway has struck! But, sadly, no one is there to share in your triumphant recollection of one of the campiest and creepiest music videos of all time.

You're not a genius when you figure things out in the shower—and there is nothing funky about the chemical make-up of the soap—it's all about neurons. But it is also about past connections, past influences, and past collaborations.

A comprehensive review of the neuroscience of memory and recall is—as they say—*beyond the scope of this work*. Nonetheless, many would argue that memories are not stored in our brains fully formed; they are neurologically constructed each time we draw upon them. As we reconstruct the past, we can also build upon it, adding a new layer or dimension. We literally build upon the past when we reconstruct what we already know in new ways. But we cannot make these advancements in our thinking—whether that be a new artistic style or the solution to what to get our spouse for our upcoming anniversary—without having past experiences. Ideation builds upon past information.

Even when it appears that we are inventing on our own, our past experiences are always with us. Creativity is always socially and culturally distributed. And oftentimes, the social nature is quite obvious, as young people connect with others to develop ideas within a given teaching and learning environment or make explicit connections with others outside of that teaching and learning environment as they engage in the work of invention and innovation.

Biography of an Idea

Reframing creativity as the biography of an idea makes visible the various actors who have contributed to the development of that idea—in unique ways—over time.

Let's play a game: Think of a creative icon. Anybody at all. Somebody who is held up as a sort of gamechanger or hero or genius. It could be an artist, a scientist, a political activist, a designer, or even an athlete. We're Americans, so we are going to throw out some examples from our culture: Taylor Swift, Michael Jackson, Barack Obama, LeBron James, Toni Morrison, Henry Ford, Margaret Mead, Dr. Martin Luther King, Jr., Ann Hutchinson, and Harry Houdini. We're swinging for the fences here, and being intentionally controversial (at times) on purpose. You can come up with your own list of a few names of supposedly creative individuals. Once you do, the fun begins.

Choose one.

Got it?

Now that you have that creative icon in mind, try to see beyond the mystique of their eminence or celebrity, and really try to understand what is the creative idea that they are most known for—not their best album or speech or theorem but the greater idea that underlies their work. What is the history of this idea? Who are the various people who have also contributed to the development of this idea? And how might they have uniquely contributed?

As an example let's go with Martin Luther King. Many people would argue that he was a good guy, he stood for good things, and he was brave and courageous, a leader among men (and women). Some might say that his greatest work was his moving "I Have a Dream" speech that he gave on the March on Washington for Jobs and Freedom on August 28, 1963. While that was indeed a momentous speech, it can also be viewed as a sole artifact in the broader idea of the Civil Rights Movement and the effort to end a long history of racism in America. These ideas persist today, and many other actors have played a role in them since Dr. King did in the 1960s, just as many other actors played a role in these ideas concurrently with Dr. King and even before he came on the scene.

To be clear, we're not trying to take anything away from Dr. King. We have deep respect for him and for all he did to advance the conversation on civil rights in the United States. Our intention here is to make the point—that if we retell the biography of a supposedly creative individual as the biography of an idea that individual is most known for, we will see that many people have participated in the development of that idea over time—in a variety of ways. In this case, if rather than explore the life history—or biography—of Dr. King, we explore the history of the Civil Rights Movement in America, we'll see that many individuals contributed to the biography of this idea—each in their own unique way.

Yes, it was bold, brave, and beautiful for Dr. King to stand on the steps of the Lincoln Memorial and offer his "I Have a Dream" speech, but if we overemphasize Dr. King and this big moment when teaching American history, many young people may shirk away, be intimidated, or not see themselves as capable of engaging in creative work. If we instead explore the story of the Civil Rights Movement more broadly and describe how many people participated in that movement in ways that may have been less pronounced, then young people will see that they too can contribute to creative idea development in their own unique ways.

In the creative classroom, it is important to foreground the social nature of ideas and to make visible the ways in which ideas evolve over time and take shape through the contributions of others. Even when it appears that an idea has emerged as the result of one person's individual thinking, that young people and adults appear to be acting independently, their process of ideation can always be traced back to past collaborations. Mapping out the social origins of ideas is helpful in understanding how an idea has evolved over time and who has participated in its development along the way.

Importance of Role

People play various roles when they participate in creative idea development.

Have you ever had this experience: you're on a bus or a train or even in an elevator car with a small collection of people that you have never met before, you get stuck for a brief moment for some unknown reason, and then you think to yourself—*What if when the doors to this thing open, we'll all walk into a dystopian drama and the small collection of people on this [bus, train, elevator car, whatever] will have to build a new world together? What roles will each of us play?*[14]

You'll often find that in the prototypical plot to a dystopian drama where a collection of strangers are suddenly and quite unexpectedly thrust into a survival-based problem-solving scenario together, the oddball group of folks within this mix hail from many different backgrounds and have many different backstories and that each of them has something to offer to the challenge that is in front of them. We admit it. That's like the plot to the television series *Lost* and a thousand other science fiction stories. Yes, that might be a weird lens through which to see the world, but, really, sometimes in those situations... don't *you* think that?

OK, so engaging your students in participatory creativity shouldn't necessarily be like inviting them into a dystopian drama—but there are similarities. Go with us here...

In the dystopian drama, the ragtag group of survivors have some creative work in front of them. It will be hard work, it will take place over time, and it will require that various people play a variety of roles in order to get that work done. But the challenge presented to these folks is not just about one thing they need to make or do. There is a bigger idea that holds the plot together— the idea of creating a new world order or repopulating the Earth or defeating a zombie army—and multiple things that will be made and done to pursue the development of this creative idea. While the characters in this dystopian drama pursue the development of some wild idea, they will inevitably draw upon their many and varied past experiences—and their rich cultural identities—to develop this idea together. Race, religion, gender identity, and a host of values laden within a wealth of life histories will all go into the mix.

Yes, it is true, the prototypical plot for a dystopian drama is internationally set up to create this kind of narrative based around diversity—and also around, well, drama. But what is also true is that any collection of people in any sort of scenario can come together to build on their past experiences, skill sets, and expertise to engage in creative problem-solving—or in the development of creative ideas.

Here, the importance of role shines through.

In the Popular Pitfalls and Misconceptions section of this chapter, we note that the everybody-doing-everything-together approach to creativity (also known as collaboration) is rarely productive. We have also noted previously that creative idea development takes more than just one type of cognitive capacity, more than just one type of meaning-making, more than just one skill set, and more than just one set of cultural perspectives and background experiences. Diversity is a key element to creative idea development—and, in this way, diversity is central to the importance that roles play in creative learning experiences.

Creative idea development takes many people from many different backgrounds bringing with them many different perspectives and holding many different talents and abilities. All of those elements are essential to the development of creative ideas. And we know, when you show up to teach your third-period class on a Wednesday morning or when you show up to teach that museum education class on a Saturday afternoon, you have not carefully engineered what students will be there and what attributes they will bring to your creative teaching and learning environment. The kids in the room are the kids in the room. Just like in the dystopian drama—no one planned for there to be a plane crash on a lush tropical island riddled with monsters—but the surviving passengers are who they are, and they each bring something to the table, and they will all find important roles to play in their greater mission.

When students participate in creativity, they naturally take on particular roles that are best suited to the demands of the task at hand and their own strengths. But as the roles that students play in the creative classroom come into greater relief, it is important for educators to remember that young people and adults are multidimensional.

Rather than narrowly define students and place them into participatory boxes, educators must understand how each participant in the creative classroom contributes to the idea development process in unique ways.

Profiles of Participation

> *Young people and adults play different roles when they participate in the development of creative ideas, but those roles are neither fixed nor unidimensional but rather multiple and dynamic.*

During the 1980s, our Project Zero colleague Howard Gardner wrote an exciting book called *Frames of Mind,* which changed the way many people thought about the concept of intelligence.[15] In this book, Howard proposed the Theory of Multiple Intelligences. This new theory suggested that people are smart in not just one way but rather many different ways. Educators were drawn to this new theory of the intelligences because it made clear something that so many of them had known for so long: that not every kid is intelligent in the same way. With all due respect to educators and their enthusiasm for this new framing of the intelligences, it was unfortunately the case that many people misinterpreted Howard. Instead of viewing students as each having a multiplicity of intelligences, some educators began to pigeonhole their students and put them into boxes, suggesting that Jimmy is a logical-mathematical learner, Maria is a visual-spatial learner, and Raheem is an interpersonal learner. And that's not entirely what Howard meant.

Yes, Jimmy, Maria, and Raheeem may be intelligent in all of these ways, but they are intelligent in other ways as well.

In some of his later work, Howard wrote about a concept he referred to as a *profile of intelligence.*[16] What he wisely argued for here was that all young people and adults are intelligent in each of the many different ways that he first described but in different amounts. The effort here was to move people away from pigeonholing young people and putting them into cognitive boxes.

Not all people are intelligent or smart in the same way; instead, each individual possesses a unique profile of intelligence, taking into account their cognitive strengths and weaknesses. By extension, not all people have the potential to participate in creativity in the same way. It may be true that in the creative classroom Jimmy might be drawn to the mathematical aspects of the work,

Maria may take the lead on design, and Raheem might be the primary social negotiator with an astute sense of empathy and a knack for making sure everyone gets along, but Jimmy, Maria, and Raheem likely participate in the development of ideas in a variety of other ways as well.

Identifying the profiles of participation for each student in the creative classroom further avails educators the opportunity to understand the dimensionality of their students and tap students' potential—or to challenge students to stretch beyond their comfort zones in unexpected ways. Making visible each student's profile of participation is a safeguard against limiting their potential in the creative classroom, just as it is a means for young people to see that (a) they have something valuable to offer during creative learning experiences and (b) there are many ways that they can participate in the development of creative ideas.

Popular Pitfalls and Misconceptions

The original *Participatory Creativity* book was published in 2016. Since then, we have had the privilege and good fortune to share this work with a variety of educators in many different settings. Sometimes the shape of this sharing has been through keynote presentations or interactive workshops offered at large conferences; sometimes the shape of this sharing has been through small working groups, online courses, or even casual conversations with friends in the staff room, at a dinner engagement, or during happy hour. We have found that, for the uninitiated, sometimes the concept of participatory creativity can be difficult to grasp in its full dimensionality. Whether scholars, educators, or moms and dads with a lot on their minds, many people have preconceived notions about creativity in general, and the concept of participatory creativity may challenge those preconceived notions.

Over the years, we have collected a list of what we call the *popular pitfalls and misconceptions* about participatory creativity. In many cases, these pitfalls and misconceptions have surfaced from the questions we have received at the end of a conference presentation or a thoughtful social interaction. In other cases, these pitfalls and misconceptions have surfaced from our own intuition about what may be tricky to understand about participatory creativity and may need more clarity.

In this section, we attend to the popular pitfalls and misconceptions surrounding participatory creativity, dispelling myths and providing a nuanced understanding of its principles. For those of you reading this book cover to cover, what appears below may feel a little repetitive given what you've read in the pages before. We like to think of it more along the lines of offering a recap of some finer points that may not have been highlighted above. We also like to think that this section may support you in the future, as you present the idea of participatory creativity to your friends, funders, and colleagues—giving you some important talking points to respond to those frequently asked questions.

Underscoring the Value of the Individual

While participatory creativity emphasizes collective engagement, it also recognizes and values the unique contributions of individuals. In fact, participatory creativity makes a firm effort to highlight the unique talents, skills, background experiences, and social and cultural perspectives that each person has to offer in a creative learning experience. Individuals make up collectives, and it is the richness, uniqueness, and diversity of the individuals who engage in creative learning experiences that propel socially distributed creative idea development forward.

Don't Call It Collaboration!

Collaboration is often simply understood as everyone doing everything together all at once. Collaboration may also be used to describe group work: young people or adults working together to solve a problem, address a task, or make something, fix something, or build something new. Simple understandings of collaboration as such limit the opportunities for young people to bring the best of their individual selves to the work at hand. By contrast, participatory creativity emphasizes the various roles that young people play when they contribute to the development of creative ideas.[17]

More than Group Work

Related to the point above, participatory creativity is more than group work. Throughout the participatory creativity process, do young people work in small groups? Yes, they often do. But participatory creativity is meant to extend the work of socially distributed idea development beyond the interaction of a few students working within close proximity to one another. Instead, it is meant to take a broader systems-based approach to invention and innovation that considers a larger set of contributors that reach beyond just a few kids sitting around a table. Participatory creativity may not even require the face-to-face interaction of young people in small groups and may instead take the form of virtual connections, community engagement, or any number of other implicit or explicit interactions. Ultimately, participatory creativity extends beyond simple group dynamics and fosters deeper connections, collective intelligence, and the shared engagement of ideas.

Participating in Creativity—All by Oneself

Participatory creativity does not necessarily require young people to be working in groups together all the time. The creative process is often supported by young people working together, taking time to work separately as individuals, and then coming back together again. That being said, participatory creativity does not require young people to work in traditional small groups at all. The individual student engaged on their own can just as easily participate in creativity by drawing upon their past experiences or remotely connecting with a community of practice. What's helpful here is to support young people in understanding—and making visible—how they are participating in creativity. Even when they appear to be by themselves, they are never truly working alone.

Is This All about Extroverts?

Participatory creativity embraces and values the strengths and contributions of both extroverts and introverts—and all of the in-between-overts who live in the middle. It is true that in many group learning experiences, quieter students may struggle to have their voices heard. But participatory creativity is not just about group work. The skilled educator will seek opportunities to establish inclusive environments for diverse personalities and find pathways for her more introverted students to participate in creativity—which may or may not involve directly working with a small group of students in the traditional sense. Surfacing each individual student's profile of participation may help in this regard—showing how each student, regardless of how quiet or pronounced their presence may be, has something valuable to offer to the process of socially distributed idea development.

Labeling Kids and Putting Them in Boxes

Young people play different roles when they participate in socially distributed idea development, but those roles should never be thought of as being fixed or unidimensional. Instead, the roles young people play in the creative classroom should be viewed as being multiple and dynamic. Supporting young people in developing their own unique profiles of participation is beneficial here, as it makes visible to them the many ways that they can contribute to the development of creative ideas—and may even challenge them to find new ways to participate in creativity that stretch beyond their profile of participation. Ultimately, participatory creativity celebrates the unique talents and potential of every young person, moving beyond limiting labels and nurturing a growth mindset.

Making Visible vs. Measuring, Assessing, and Testing

Participatory creativity focuses on making creative processes and outcomes visible rather than solely measuring and testing young people on a limited set of cognitive capacities. By telling the biography of an idea of a student-generated project, students and their teachers have the opportunity to show how a variety of young people contributed to the development of the idea they have been working on over time, what unique and varied roles they played, whom else they engaged in the process, and what they have learned along the way. When educators highlight the social emergent nature of creative idea development, taking a participatory approach to creativity has the potential to shift assessment practices to capture the multifaceted dimensions of invention and innovation.

What about "Giftedness" and "Talent"?

Young people who are labeled as "gifted and talented" according to traditional standards are often designated as such under a narrow set of cognitive measures that privilege some ways of meaning-making over others. Such young people have much to offer in the creative classroom, but so too do other students who make sense of the world differently—and who likewise have much to offer throughout the process of socially distributed idea development. While we do not outright reject the very notion of gifted-and-talented curricula (indeed, many teachers do much good work in these settings), we do find it challenging. As opposed to gifted-and-talented learning experiences that offer high-level learning experiences for a select few students, a participatory approach to creativity can provide opportunities for all individuals, including those traditionally labeled as gifted or talented, to engage, contribute, and develop their creative capacities and profiles of participation.

Look Beyond the Arts Bias

The arts classroom—whether that be music, theater, visual art, dance, the literary arts, or any number of other arts forms from a variety of cultural traditions—is certainly a place that is ripe for participatory creativity. But so too is the design studio, the fab lab, the makerspace, or any other learning environment where things are built and designed. But even beyond these spaces, participatory creativity can take place. In fact, we firmly take a disciplinary agnostic approach to the application of participatory creativity and believe that participatory creativity can be enacted in any teaching and learning environment. We challenge the bias that creativity of any sort is exclusive to the arts; instead, we assert that engagement in creative idea development can take place in any discipline and in any teaching and learning context.[18]

Don't Think of a Light Bulb!

Images of light bulbs are deeply associated with the idea of creative insight. A quick image search of creativity in education will yield a wealth of examples. Despite this association, we find the connection between light bulbs and creativity to be highly misleading. Light bulbs suggest that creativity manifests itself in sudden flashes of insight that are often described as *a-ha* moments. While we agree that a-ha moments exist (see the discussion of *l'esprit de l'escalier* earlier in this chapter), we also believe that creativity takes place over time and involves purposeful work. Participatory creativity emphasizes the iterative nature of the creative process, encouraging ongoing engagement, exploration, and transformation by an array of contributors. Creative ideas wend their way in the world over the course of time and take many forms along the way. A creative idea is far more complex and lasting than a light bulb suggests.

By addressing these popular pitfalls and misconceptions, we have aimed to provide a comprehensive understanding of participatory creativity, pave the way for its effective implementation in various educational settings, pre-empt some frequently asked questions, and give you some talking points for future discussion. We hope you found them useful. In the chapter ahead, we intend to continue down the path of utility by offering some suggestions to support you in establishing a participatory creativity classroom.

Notes

1 See, for example, the popular Torrance Tests for Creative Thinking, Torrance, P. E. (2018). *Torrance tests of creative thinking: Interpretive manual*. Bensenville, IL: Scholastic Testing Services. Retrieved from https://www.ststesting.com/gift/TTCT_InterpMOD.2018.pdf

2 A full review of the literature supporting systems-based and sociocultural approaches to creativity is beyond the scope of this work. However, in the next couple of pages, we reference several scholars who have contributed to this exciting area of study. We encourage you to look to the References and Suggestions for Further Reading

section of this book to follow up on the work of any scholars or concepts mentioned in this chapter.

3 To read this manifesto, see Glăveanu, V. P., et al. (2019). Advancing creativity theory and research: A sociocultural manifesto. *Journal of Creative Behaviour*. Retrieved from: https://doi.org/10.1002/jocb.395

4 See https://participatorycreativitylab.org/

5 For a more thorough description of participation, see Clapp, E. P. (2022). Participation (encyclopedia entry). In V. P. Glăveanu (Ed.), *Palgrave encyclopedia of the possible* (pp. 966–974). Singapore: Springer Nature.

6 Two helpful resources for understanding Howard Gruber and his colleagues' concept of creativity as purposeful work are Gruber, H. E., & Wallace, D. B. (1999). The case study method and evolving systems approach for understanding unique creative people at work. In R. J. Sternberg (Ed.), *Handbook of creativity* (pp. 93–115). Cambridge, UK: Cambridge University Press, and Wallace, D. B., & Gruber, H. E. (Eds.). (1989). *Creative people at work*. Oxford, UK: Oxford University Press.

7 Many creativity theorists have written about the different variations of the letter c/C. A good place to start to understand this debate is Kaufman, J. C., & Beghetto, R. A. (2009). Beyond big and little: The four c model of creativity. *Review of General Psychology*, *13*(1), 1–2.

8 A good resource that makes this point is Glăveanu, V. P. & Clapp, E. P. (2018). Distributed and participatory creativity as a form of cultural empowerment: The role of alterity, difference, and collaboration. In A. U. Branco & M. C. Lopes-de-Oliveira (Eds.), *Alterity, values, and socialization: Human development within educational contexts* (pp. 51–63). Cham, Switzerland: Springer.

9 To learn more about the work of Lisa Delpit, you may be interested in starting with her article Delpit, L. (1988). The silenced dialogue: Power and pedagogy in educating other people's children. *Harvard Educational Review, 58*(3), 280–298 or her book Delpit, L. (2006). *Other people's children: Cultural conflict in the classroom*. New York: The New Press.

10 An introduction to social reproduction in education can be found in Bourdieu, P. & Passeron, J. (1977). *Reproduction in education, society, and culture*. Beverly Hills, CA: Sage.

11 If you want to learn more about the excellent work of our colleague Janine de Novais, check out her recent book de Novais, J. (2023). *Brave community: Teaching for a post-racist imagination*. New York: Teachers College Press.

12 Keith Sawyer once wrote that "even the insights that emerge when you're completely alone can be traced back to previous collaborations" (p. xii, 2007). We interpret this to mean that even when folks might be working by themselves, every interaction and influence that they have experienced before that moment are with them. Relatedly, our colleague Vlad Glăveanu once wrote that "even in those situations in which the artist is paints in complete solitude all the tools at his or her disposal have a social origin" (p. 37, 2014a). We interpret this to mean that, even when someone may be working by themselves, they are likely working materials or tools that other people have created and therefore communing with those other creators. The artist, in this instance, did not invent the brushes and paints that she is working with.

13 Or, perhaps more accurately, the "wit of the stairway." Many attribute the phrase *l'esprit de l'escalier* to Denis Diderot's *Paradoxe sur le Comédien* written between 1770 and 1778, posthumously published in 1830.

14 For a good time, the next time you actually get stuck on a bus, train, or elevator car with a small group of strangers, lean into one of them and present this scenario!

15 See Gardner, H. (1983). *Frames of mind: The theory of multiple intelligences.* New York, NY: Basic Books.

16 See, for example, Gardner, H. (1993). A multiplicity of intelligences. *Scientific American Presents, Exploring Intelligence, 9*(4), 19–23.

17 For more on the distinction between participatory creativity and collaboration, see Clapp, E. P. (2020). Don't call it collaboration!: Reframing success in teams from the perspective of participatory creativity. In R. Reiter-Palmon, A. McKay, & J. C. Kaufman (Eds.), *Creative success in teams.* Series: Explorations in creativity research (J. C. Kaufman, series editor) (pp. 101–121). Cambridge, MA: Academic Press.

18 To begin to explore the topic of the arts bias in creativity, see Glăveanu, V. P. (2014). Revisiting the "art bias" in lay conceptions of creativity. *Creativity Research Journal, 26*(1), 11–20.

3

Establishing a Participatory Creativity Classroom

So you've opened this book to Chapter 3—establishing a participatory creativity classroom. Welcome! Whether you're in the process of reading the book from cover to cover or you are bouncing around from chapter to chapter, we're hoping that, by arriving here, you are both interested in and curious about setting up your teaching and learning environment to support an inclusive approach to distributed idea development. Let's jump in!

What Does a Participatory Creativity Classroom Look Like?

In this chapter, we begin by exploring what a participatory creativity classroom looks like. Now, that's a very Project Zero sort of thing to do—to present a concept and describe what it looks like. To make it visible. Our colleagues at Project Zero have spent decades considering what it means to make thinking and learning visible—and have developed a wealth of tools and strategies to support students and educators in this work along the way.

Making thinking and learning visible is an interesting endeavor. It suggests taking something that is usually *in*visible and somehow bringing it into the realm of what can be seen. Developing a *documentation* practice or reviewing a student's

DOI: 10.4324/9781003136958-3

process-folio are two strategies for making student thinking and learning visible.[1] So too is developing a routine practice of looking closely at student work.[2]

Here, we are not attempting to make something intangible and invisible—like thinking and learning—visible; instead, we are aiming to shine a light on something that is quite easy to see: a classroom—albeit one of a particular sort. As simple to see as a classroom may be, we're intentionally not going to illustrate too clear a picture of what a participatory creativity classroom looks like. Instead, we're going to mix things up a little bit by constructing more of a collage than a photorealistic painting.

So what does a participatory creativity classroom look like? Sometimes a participatory creativity classroom looks like young people up and about, moving around, accessing different parts of the room. Sometimes it looks like young people working with interesting tools and materials. Sometimes those tools and materials are all different. Sometimes they are all the same. Sometimes there is music involved in the participatory creativity classroom. There are instruments being twanged, banged, plucked, blown, and strummed. Sometimes it is loud. Sometimes it is not. Sometimes there are students huddled together around a table. Sometimes those students are sketching, making lists, or mind mapping with markers and chart paper. Sometimes they are writing on white boards, writing on walls, writing on windows. And of course—sometimes there are Post-it Notes, but oftentimes there are not. Sometimes there is technology: laptops, desktops, tablets, smartphones, virtual reality (VR) goggles, and other gadgetry. Sometimes the technology is significantly less technological—like paper, pencil, pens, and paints. Sometimes the participatory creativity classroom looks like a baseball field, a soccer field, a basketball court, an ice rink, or a swimming pool— there may be bats, balls, helmets, or hoops. Sometimes the participatory creativity classroom looks more like a playground, a sandbox, a doll house, a balance beam, or a ropes course. And sometimes the participatory creativity classroom does not look or feel like a physical space at all. It's a virtual space where young people from around the corner and around the globe converge to build ideas together. Physical or virtual, sometimes these spaces erupt in laughter. The participatory creativity classroom looks like smiles on children's faces, curiosity and wonder in young people's eyes. But sometimes the participatory creativity classroom looks like strict concentration, furrowed brows, or the frustration of a failed effort. Every now and then, the participatory creativity classroom may even look like a pile of crumpled pieces of paper ringing the base of a garbage can, a prototype broken in two after having crashed to the floor. But most of the time—a participatory creativity classroom looks like joy.

We can go on and on, but the point we're trying to make here has likely already been made. That is, the participatory creativity classroom does not look one specific way. It may look many different ways, take many different forms, and even change forms from moment to moment (see Figure 3.1). And while we are not ruling it out—a form that the participatory creativity classroom usually does not take is the form of students sitting in rows, staring up at the front of the room where an educator in an authority position is expounding their knowledge in front of a chalkboardwhiteboardsmartboardslideprojector. But like we said, we're not entirely ruling that out. The occasional lecture has its place—even in the participatory creativity classroom.

Any Classroom Can Be a Participatory Creativity Classroom

First things first: we want to make it clear that any classroom can be a participatory creativity classroom. Sure, the art studio, theater, makerspace, and design lab are natural contenders to be learning spaces where participatory creativity takes place. "Kids doing creative stuff together—must be an arts, design, or maker sorta space," one might say. And they would be right! Environments where creation and collaboration have traditionally taken place are ripe for the work of participatory creativity, but so too are any number of other classrooms. Classrooms where the core content areas are taught can be environments for participatory creativity just as much as any other space.

FIGURE 3.1 The participatory creativity classroom can take many different forms. Illustration by Julie Rains.

But sometimes the participatory creativity classroom is not even a classroom. It's a museum, a garden, a kitchen, grandpa's work shed, the library, the field out back, or a space between spaces. Anywhere that young people or adults are coming together, either in person or virtually, to develop creative ideas together can be a participatory creativity classroom.

Consider the Context

OK, so you've read this far into Chapter 3 and what you have deduced is that the participatory creativity classroom does not look like one thing; it may look like many things. You've also deduced that any learning environment can be a participatory creativity classroom. The logic model here is starting to feel a little bit like everything is anything and anything is everything. And that circular reasoning may not be giving you a whole lot of direction. So… you may be wondering right about now if things will ever start to get concrete. The answer is *yes*.

The specifics of the participatory creativity classroom matter. Whether you're working in a lecture hall, a lunch room, a science lab, or a soccer field, considering the context is elemental to engaging learners in the work of participatory creativity. Here, we do not mean to denude a learning environment of what makes it unique and then set it up in a wholly new way. Instead, we want to celebrate the uniqueness of a learning environment by considering all of its attributes from an assets-based perspective.

Where are You?

First, consider where your classroom lives in the world. Where is your classroom in relation to the broader school or organization it may be housed in? Where is that school or organization situated within the broader neighborhood and community? What is the relationship between the school or organization and the neighborhood? What is unique about this neighborhood? And what are the affordances of this particular part of the world? This is where you are. Understanding the broader landscape within which your classroom is situated is the first step you can take toward building on all that that landscape may have to offer. Of course, you can always take a "challenges and opportunities" approach to understanding this landscape, but we find it far more useful to take an "assets and affordances" approach. Where am I? What's unique about this place? What's possible here?

What Have You Got?

Second, consider what resources are at your disposal. Within your classroom, what furniture do you have, how is that furniture

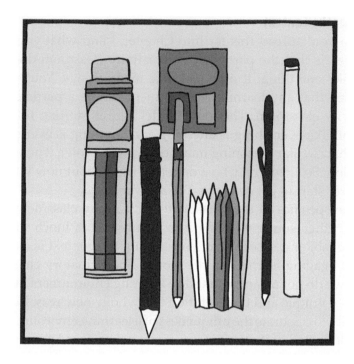

FIGURE 3.2 The materials you have access to are part of the context that you are in. It is important to take an assets-based approach to what you've got.

Illustration by Julie Rains.

set up? What technology do you have? What are the surfaces like? Where are the windows? What sort of lighting is in place. What kind of *stuff* is in your room? Are there tools or materials? Are there stacks of paper and books on shelves? Consider the same for the broader school or organization you are in. What sort of stuff do you have access to? What sort of spaces do you have access to? You can further consider the same for the broader neighborhood and community. What kind of stuff is here? This is what you've got. What are the assets and affordances of the stuff you have access to?

Who Are You Working With?

Lastly, but most importantly, consider who are the people you will be working with. If you are going to be taking a participatory approach to distributed idea development, then the participants involved in that experience are indeed the most essential part! Here, it is important to do some deep work to understand who are the young people and adults you will be working with in your classroom, in your broader school or organization, and within the wider neighborhood and community. Where do these people come from? What are their roles within the community? What are their beliefs, cultural heritage practices, and traditions? Do the individuals in your classroom and your community represent a particular social, cultural, ethnic, or financial community or tradition? What is the nature of those communities or traditions? What are the things that bring them together as a community? What brings them joy? But also, what are the things that challenge them as a community? What causes them to pause, reflect, and be silent and still? Beyond considering who they are as a unit, you should consider who they are as individuals. What flavor of richness does each individual learner or creative partner bring to the work of distributed idea development? What are the assets and affordances of this collective tribe you are now a part of—and what are the assets and affordances of the very unique individual members who make up that tribe? These are the people you will be working with. They are your most precious assets and affordances. How can you celebrate, support, leverage, lean into, and elevate each one of them?

At the same time, it is important to consider who you are in relation to this community and this context. Are you an insider, an outsider, or an in-between-sider? And what does that even mean? (We'll discuss this more at the end of this chapter, but just make a note here: it's important stuff!)

The Where, the What, and the Who

By considering the context of your teaching and learning environment in the way that we have described above, you first inquire and then understand where you are, what you've got, and who you will be working with. This is where you are, this is what you've got, this is who you will be working with. And that's exciting! Taking such an assets- and affordances-based approach will help you see the richness to be found within your context—and will help you find the best ways to engage your learners in the pursuit of participatory creativity.

FIGURE 3.3 When establishing a participatory creativity classroom, you should consider the context—including the setting, resources, and people you have access to.

Illustration by Julie Rains.

Flexibility Is Key

Whether you are an insider or an outsider to the classroom you have entered, in order to make this shared learning environment a participatory creativity place—flexibility is key.

Flexibility begins with considering the context of your classroom. One might say it is about being *responsive* to where you are, what you've got, and who you are working with, but being responsive can sound a little bit like being *reactive*. And being reactive can sound a lot like solving problems or dealing with issues. Instead, we would argue that being flexible with where you are, what you got, and what you are working with is more like throwing a party. And parties can happen anywhere under any set of conditions. The people, the place, and the stuff at your disposal will bring the party. Some people may refer to these three variables as your *constraints*. Sure, to be fair, where you are, what you've got, and who you are working with can be viewed as constraints—and there has been a lot written about creativity and constraints[3]—but we don't view where you are, what you've got, and who you are working with as being constraining at all. Instead, we see these three aspects of classroom context as the makings of deeper learning, inquiry, a good time, and an inclusive experience wherein each person brings their best for the benefit of the greater experience—your participatory creativity party.

There is a saying that comes from the principles of Open Space Technology: *the people who are here are the right people to be here.*[4] We believe that. But we further believe that we can extend this positive outlook on communities coming together to say that the spaces we occupy and the stuff that we have are the right spaces and the right stuff to engage in during a participatory creativity learning experience. Combined, where you are, what you got, and who you are working with bring the party.

Aside from throwing a party, another way of thinking about flexibility in the participatory creativity classroom has to do with following ideas wherever they lead. In Melbourne, Australia, an elementary school teacher named Naomi was once working with her students on a unit about climate change. The concept of greenhouse gasses casually came up during one of her lessons. A student raised their hand to ask what a greenhouse gas was. Soon, many students became interested in what a greenhouse gas may be. Naomi then shifted her lesson to follow the students' interest. What resulted from this experience was the "Surface a Wonder, Follow a Wonder" tool that you will find in Chapter 5 of this book. Following student wonder is an important way of exercising flexibility in the participatory creativity classroom. Surfacing wonder is helpful, but so too is providing the open space for ideas to emerge and then the freedom and flexibility for students to pursue the development of those ideas within the structure of a given learning experience.

The 12 Practices of Participatory Creativity

Another interest we have for this chapter is to provide direction for educators wishing to establish a participatory creativity classroom. To that end, our goal in the pages ahead is not so much to present a checklist for establishing a classroom setting that fosters participatory creativity but rather to offer a suite of suggestions for ways to engage young people within the practice of distributed idea development. We call these the 12 practices of participatory creativity. Our intention here is to be useful to educators who are interested in getting started with participatory creativity, without being too prescriptive.

Identify the Opportunity Space(s)

It is our belief that participatory creativity can happen in any content area and in any classroom. Indeed, in Chapter 4, we will share a variety of curricular contexts where participatory creativity has taken place. An essential step toward establishing a participatory creativity classroom is identifying the opportunity space for this work to occur. Within the content area you teach, where might there be opportunities for young people to develop or explore ideas together? What might be some interesting inquiries for young people to pursue, and how might you provide space within your curriculum for young people to pursue those inquiries?

Home in on Ideas

At the heart of participatory creativity is the development of creative ideas. Homing in on ideas is therefore a key part of developing a participatory creativity practice. For you as an educator, this may mean shifting your focus away from products to support your students in engaging in the rich exploration of ideas. It may also mean finding throughlines in your curriculum that your students may pursue. Above all, an important participatory creativity pedagogical move that you can make may be to explicitly focus your students on the idea of an idea—how ideas develop over time and how your students may participate in the development of interesting ideas.

Look Backward to Go Forward

In many approaches to innovation, there is a strong emphasis on designing something new—without looking backward to see what's been done before. From the perspective of participatory creativity, exploring past histories to find new opportunities is key. Looking forward without looking back can be very limiting and may yield lost opportunities or limited results. Participatory creativity indeed concerns itself with novelty, but it firmly situates novelty within the evolution of longer standing narratives. Equipping young people with the skill of looking backward to go forward is therefore a primary practice of creative idea development.

Emphasize Roles

Young people and adults play various roles when they contribute to the development of creative ideas. As you engage with the students in your classroom, consider the various roles they may play in the creative process. It may be helpful here to be explicit with your students about the importance of roles in the creative process. This may be especially helpful for young people and adults who hold more traditional views on creativity. It may further open your students up to understanding that there is not one way, but multiple ways, that they can participate in the development of creative ideas.

Find an On-ramp for Everyone

Taking a participatory approach to creativity suggests not only that multiple people contribute to the development of creative ideas but also that there is a role for everyone to play in the idea development process. While the dream is that young people will find their own ways into this process, it is helpful for you, as an educator, to consider the strengths that each of your students may bring to the participatory creativity classroom and, whenever necessary, to find on-ramps and inroads for each of your students to engage in during the process of distributed idea development. All of your students have unique roles to play in the creative process! Keep in mind here that each young person may play various roles in the idea development process and be

FIGURE 3.4 Consider the various roles that young people (and adults) may play within your participatory creativity classroom.

Illustration by Julie Rains.

sure not to pigeonhole one or another student as being restricted to participate in creativity in a single way.

Consider Multiple Perspectives

No one would argue that the development of creative ideas can only get better with the input of people holding different perspectives. Being proactive about incorporating multiple perspectives into the creative idea process will benefit the work of your students (see Figure 3.5). It's also a great habit to instill at an early age—that young people should look beyond their own perspective and consider the perspectives of others (especially people who may think very differently from them).

Foreground Diversity

No one would further argue that the development of creative ideas can only get better with diversity. Yeah, we get it, diversity can mean a lot of things. And here we are trying to embrace as many of those lots of things as possible. As your students

FIGURE 3.5 Being proactive about incorporating multiple perspectives into the creative idea process will benefit the work of your students.

Illustration by Julie Rains.

are engaging in the process of creative idea development, are girls working with boys? Are LGTBQ+ kids working with hetero kids? Is there social, racial, cultural, and religious diversity within small groups? Is that guy on the football team working with the kids in the emo band? Diversity looks different in each of our classrooms. To the degree that it is possible, encourage diversity across the idea development process and support your students in understanding the value of diversity in the creative process—and in life.

Tap the Community

It is rarely the case that all of the knowledge and expertise that are necessary to engage in the development of creative ideas lives within the classroom. To this end, encourage your students to tap the wisdom of their communities when engaging in the process of creative idea development. What is a community? That could be the classroom, the school, or the neighborhood—or beyond. Doesn't Ilya's grandmother make amazing empanadas? Isn't that guy down the block always working on really cool dirt bikes? And what's up with those college kids who are always launching something that look like weather balloons into the air? When tapping the community, encourage your students to seek out perspectives of folks who may see or experience the world differently from themselves.

Think, Make, Do (and Do Again)

Whether participatory or otherwise, the creative process is rarely a straight line or a one-and-done experience. Set your students up for trial and error by encouraging them to think, make, do— and do again.[5] Iterate! Iterate! Iterate!

Document and Reflect

In step with iteration are the related topics of documentation and reflection. Throughout the idea development process, encourage your students to document their thinking and to frequently reflect on their experiences by reviewing their documentation. By developing a practice for documentation and reflection, your students will in turn develop data to support the biographies of the ideas they are pursuing. Along the way, they will see the twists and turns that their idea development process has taken— and find new pathways forward based on their past efforts.

Tell the Story

Don't let all of that rich documentation go to waste! Encourage your students to tell the story of their idea development process. When they do, urge your students to share their starts and stops as much as their successes. We have just as much (if not more) to learn from our failed attempts as we do from the things that worked well. Have your students tell the story of their idea development process often. Routinizing the storytelling of a creative idea will help students to think in terms of where they have been and what they might do next—while opening them up to receive feedback and suggestions from their peers. It's also an important way for your students to make their thinking and learning visible(ish)—and to show how their story fits into other stories of idea development within the domain in which they are working.

Don't Forget Joy

It's fair to say that the development of creative ideas does not happen without struggle. It's also fair to say that the development of creative ideas should be rooted in joy. Participatory creative learning experiences can foster the thrill of developing new ideas in the company of others, the pride of understanding how one's individual agency can contribute to a greater goal, and the joy involved in participating in the process of change. If you design a participatory creativity learning experience for nothing else, design it for joy.

According to Whom, for Whom, and Who Am I?

We would like to offer you one last piece of advice for establishing a participatory creativity classroom: develop a habit of having a critical lens on the history of ideas. When young people encounter new ideas or innovations, encourage them to ask *according to whom? for whom?* and *who am I?* These are the critical lenses for progressive education that Edward and his colleagues developed while teaching a class about Project Zero practices at the Harvard Graduate School of Education.[6] These critical lenses ask us to consider who may have been involved in the development of a particular idea or innovation—and what perspectives they may have brought to that work.

No idea or innovation is socially or culturally neutral, even if it is presented as such. While not always easy to ascertain, ideas and innovations are laden with the values of the individuals who contributed to their development. Understanding where ideas and innovations come from by looking closely and critically at their past histories is important as we consider their adoption—or how we may contribute to their next chapters.

It's also important to understand what the original purpose or audience for a given idea or innovation may have been. When encountering a given idea or innovation, it is helpful to support the young people in your classroom to think critically about the original purpose or target audience for this idea or innovation. Do your students look the same or different from the original target audience of the ideas or innovations that they are working with? Are they interested in using the ideas or innovations they are working with in the same way that they were originally intended? How might an idea or innovation be adapted or changed to serve the interests of your students? What might be the social, cultural, or political implications of tweaking an idea or innovation for a new audience—or for a new purpose?

Perhaps most importantly, when establishing a participatory creativity classroom, it is helpful to instill within your students (and yourself!) the work of reflective practice.

Reflective wha…?

When we engage in the process of reflective practice, we consider bringing our whole selves to a teaching and learning—or creativity—experience.[7] This includes who we are as educated folks in the world and all of the formal and informal schooling we've experienced in the past, but it also includes all of the elements that make up our identities—that might be the usual markers of identity, like race, class, religion, and sexual orientation, but it also includes all of the experiences we've had that have made us the people we are today. Being aware of who we are as individuals helps us in myriad ways in the participatory creativity classroom. It helps us understand our relationship to the content we are working with; it helps us understand what we might offer, what roles we might play, and what perspectives we may share in the idea development process; and it compels us to consider what we know, what we don't know—what are our blind spots?—and how we might connect with others to move an idea or innovation forward.

And that's it! Our goal for this chapter has been to provide some pointers for how to establish a participatory creativity classroom. We started out offering a bricolage-like picture of what the participatory creativity classroom may look like and then moved on to offer 12 pedagogical practices to support participatory creativity in your classroom. We closed the show by offering critical lenses for engaging in this work. As stated above, our intention here is not to be prescriptive but rather to be suggestive in moves you might make in doing this exciting work. We hope that this chapter has pushed this book into the realm of the practical—and we hope you have found it useful. In the coming chapter, we'll move further in the direction of practicality by sharing a wealth of examples of participatory creativity in action.

Notes

1 For more about developing a documentation practice, see Krechevsky, M., Mardell, B., Rivard, M., & Wilson, D. (2013). *Visible learners: Promoting Reggio-inspired approaches in all schools*. San Francisco, CA: Jossey-Bass. For more about process-folios, see Winner, E. (1991). *Arts PROPEL: An introductory handbook*. Educational Testing Service and Presidents and Fellows of Harvard College.

2 For more about looking closely at student work, see Blythe, T., Allen, D., & Powell, B. S. (1999). *Looking together at student work*. New York: Teachers College Press.

3 See, for example, Tromp, C. (in press). *The power of creative constraints*. New York: Oxford University Press, and Rodriguez, B. (2017). *The power of creative constraints (TED talk)*. Retrieved from https://ed.ted.com/lessons/the-power-of-creative-constraints-brandon-rodriguez

4 For more on Open Space Technology, see Owen, H. (n.d.). *A brief user's guide to open space technology*. Retrieved from https://openspaceworld.org/wp2/hho/papers/brief-users-guide-open-space-technology/

5 For more about an inspirational version of the iterative concept of think, make, do, see Gary Stager and Sylvia Liobow Martinez's book *Invent to Learn*.

6 To learn more about these questions and their origin story, see Clapp, E. P., & Kamilah, A. (2019). Critical lenses for progressive education. In: M. Peters & R. Heraud (Eds.), *Encyclopedia of educational innovation*. Singapore: Springer. https://doi.org/10.1007/978-981-13-2262-4_109-1. Special thanks to Carrie James for the development of these ideas.

7 For more about reflective practice, see the Envisioning Innovation for Education toolkit for Professional Development.

4

Participatory Creativity in Action

In a technology classroom in South Korea, young people consider the human needs associated with the gadgets and gizmos in their lives in order to experiment with innovations for future applications of a variety of technological tools. In the suburbs of Cleveland, Ohio, an educator uses his yerba mate cup to support his students in systems thinking. Meanwhile, in Melbourne, Australia, an educator works with his students to develop a tool for self and peer assessment to help make their profiles of participation visible.

If you are arriving at Chapter 4 after reading from the beginning of this book, you'll know that we've offered a crash course in participatory creativity and then provided suggestions for establishing a participatory creativity classroom. Here, we dive into the real-world implementation of participatory creativity in classrooms. Through a series of stories and examples, we explore how educators from various contexts have embraced participatory creativity and its transformative potential. In the pages ahead, we're excited to offer a window into what participatory creativity looks like in action by sharing a variety of *pictures of practice*. What's a picture of practice? Think of it as a mini–case study, a look into the work of an idea in action.

The pictures of practice we share below each illustrate a different aspect of the participatory creativity framework. We like to think that they each have their own character, and while we've

DOI: 10.4324/9781003136958-4

set up something of a structure, they all take on their own shape and form. To construct these pictures of practice, we reached out to the greater community of educators engaged in the work of participatory creativity. Many of the folks mentioned below are close professional colleagues of ours—whereas others are new friends that we have met through this project. To tell the stories that we do, we connected with the folks who are celebrated in the coming pages to engage in casual interviews which were carefully transcribed and analyzed. We then went to work writing up each narrative, oftentimes checking in with our colleagues and new friends to make sure we got the story right and frequently adding details and new information.

While many of the pictures of practice shared below illustrate how an educator incorporated participatory creativity into their practice, some stories also illustrate what it looks like when young people engage in the work of participatory creativity. In some cases, it may seem like we are focusing on individuals, but in essence, each picture of practice exemplifies either the work of distributed idea development or the teaching of distributed idea development.

Each of these pictures of practice tells its own unique story. But we find it interesting to note how the community of educators represented on these pages form their own web of participatory practitioners. Even though many of the folks in this chapter may not know one another, they are connected through this work, each contributing to the greater idea of incorporating more socially distributed approaches to teaching and learning to support their students, friends, co-learners, and colleagues. That being said, the educators and young people represented in these pictures of practice have never taken a master class on participatory creativity—and they are each influenced by many other approaches to practice. So, as a reader, you may notice one or another educator or student using language that may be a little bit inconsistent with what we have presented in the previous chapters. In the spirit of participatory creativity, we think that is OK—as a blend of perspectives on pedagogy should naturally inform one's practice.

We're excited to jump into these stories! But before we do, we find it important to let you, the reader, know that some of these pictures of practice are based on conversations we had with our colleagues a few years ago. Nonetheless, we still find these stories pertinent as illustrations of participatory creativity in action. That being the case, whenever possible, we have included a *where are they now* note to celebrate the growth and development of the individuals profiled on these pages.

But enough about the details. Let's get to some stories.

Finding Future Potential in Past Histories

Joyce Lourenco Pereira shares her approach to teaching computer science in a human-centered manner, emphasizing the concepts of human needs and knowledge. She believes in the importance of empathy, collaboration, accessibility, and ethics as sub-concepts of human needs and in the importance of decisions, innovation, and data as sub-concepts of knowledge. Joyce aims to foster participatory creativity among her students by encouraging them to explore emerging technologies and their connections to these concepts.

Meet Joyce

Joyce Lourenco Pereira, originally from Brazil and now a high school design and innovation teacher at Korea International School, is a force of nature. Her positive energy and passion for teaching computer science encourage learners to uncover and trace the human stories behind innovation. Joyce believes that "Innovation is creatively using available knowledge and resources to meet human needs and enhance human experiences." And it is that emphasis on the origins of innovation that leads her learners to uncover the biographies of ideas.

For Joyce, participatory creativity is an important element in the innovation process. She explains:

Human needs are at the heart of every technological tool. Having this in mind, participatory creativity in this context helps us trace how humans throughout history have met those needs using available knowledge and resources in innovative ways. Tracing past iterations and looking closely at their benefits and limitations can help us predict and design future ones.

Joyce also notes the importance of considering diverse perspectives and viewpoints. In a recent interview with the 21st Century Learning Conference, an online streaming conference that runs all year, Joyce elaborated:

> As we invite students to trace stories of innovation, we need to consider a range of representation. There should be multicultural, multigenerational, ethnic, and gender representations in the story of innovation. I've been learning so much as I've been sharing this approach with other people about different ways different societies have met these human needs.

One area of interest that Joyce often explores with her students is telecommunication. Always thinking through the lens of diversity, Joyce and her students consider the long history of telecommunication from multiple cultural perspectives. "How have humans communicated over a distance?" she asks her students. This initial inquiry springboards a rich discussion. Joyce elaborates:

> I think my favorite iterations [of communication over distance] are pigeon carriers. I ask my students, can you imagine the human that first looked at a pigeon and said, 'You there have potential.' Someone looked at a pigeon and noticed these patterns, and when you start looking at the history of pigeon carriers, it's Egypt that was using them to really send messages. Biomimicry fascinates me, because you have to look and slow down to pay attention to things around you. Someone paid attention to a pigeon. Someone saw and noticed something, and all of a sudden, all of this potential was uncovered behind a pigeon.[1]

Joyce's Context

Joyce flashes a warm smile from the computer screen as she invites us to learn more about her approach to teaching and learning, and though we're thousands of miles away, it feels like she's across the table at a local coffee shop. Joyce teaches at Korea International School (KIS), a private school committed to innovation and the development of a strong STEAM (Science, Technology, Engineering, the Arts and Mathematics) program. With over 400 students in grades 9-12, KIS prides itself on practicing design thinking, "taking [students'] best ideas from past to present iterations."[2] As the Introduction to Artificial Intelligence, Applications Development, and AP Computer Science A teacher, Joyce is an influential actor in realizing KIS's mission. She explains, "As a woman in the field of computer science, I creatively transform the perceived chaos and complexity of this subject into order and beauty that brings joy and benefit to myself and others within my circle of influence."

To frame her courses and create that sense of order, Joyce invites her students to examine five throughlines to anchor their learning:

◆ We look to meet human needs efficiently.
◆ We trace stories of innovation to participate in designing their next iterations.
◆ We uncover patterns and trends to make informed decisions.
◆ We store data to access, manipulate, and share in creative ways.
◆ We are empowered to take action for impact within our circles of influence.

Throughout their time in Joyce's class, students will have the opportunity to examine each of these guideposts in further detail, ultimately deepening their understanding of both the realm of innovation and each other.

Joyce's Story

To get started, Joyce often begins her classes by creating a warm, inviting space for students to surface and alleviate their anxieties related to technology. With inspiration from her colleague and mentor Christine, she acknowledges that fear and uncertainty are common emotional responses to emerging technology in both her students and educator colleagues. "Even if you don't personally experience fear or uncertainty around emerging technology, I guarantee you that the people around you may be experiencing that, especially in the realm of education." Joyce emphasizes the need to address and minimize these fears, both in herself and in her students, before they can begin to uncover the origins of technological innovation. She encourages them to move toward their fears and navigate ambiguity with confidence, using inquiry-based approaches to explore and uncover complexity.

Joyce also highlights the role of empathy in understanding and solving problems related to emerging technologies. She encourages her students to find the human element behind the technology and to uncover the emotions associated with the problems worth solving. Joyce believes that by tapping into shared emotions and experiences, students can develop a deeper understanding of the impact of technology on people's lives.

To begin their exploration of the link between human needs and innovation, Joyce asks her students to generate a list of contemporary tools and apps that fulfill needs, such as water-tracking apps, food-delivery platforms, and online learning platforms. By understanding how technology can address human needs, students gain a broader perspective on the potential impact of emerging technologies.

To further engage students in participatory creativity, Joyce introduces the concept of tracing the story of innovation. She uses a template that includes four key components: (1) human needs, (2) earliest iterations, (3) meaningful iterations, and (4) current iterations (see Figure 4.1). Joyce explains to students that they can begin to document the biography of an idea by starting with any component of the framework. In other words, learners can begin by listing a recent technological iteration, like that of artificial intelligence, or by considering a human need, like the need to communicate over a distance. To further illustrate this process, Joyce shares a specific example of how this tool might be used to trace the origin of an idea.

FIGURE 4.1 Joyce Lourenco Pereira's "Story of Innovation" tool. After considering many past iterations of a particular technology through the lens of its central human need, students develop informed approaches to create the next iteration.

Illustration by Julie Rains.

Joyce begins with a current technology, virtual reality (VR). She explains that the first step is to consider the human need, which in some cases can be tricky because "sometimes the human need is not as explicit. So I would like to propose to you that virtual reality is actually a chapter in the story of humans creating immersive experiences." Joyce then invites learners to brainstorm meaningful iterations that may have happened along the way. She explains one of her initial investigations into the link between technology and human need:

> I was doing a VR unit with my students and wondering what is the human need? That's really when I started exploring technology, and then the language 'immersive experiences' surfaced in a virtual reality manual. At that moment, I realized, oh my gosh, we're storytellers. We immerse people

through our stories, through just sitting around the fire. It doesn't have to be even anything fancy. There doesn't even need to be technology. Just like, let's come around as a community and share our stories. And then I started going back and forth, recognizing that's why in the theater, they cut off all the lights.

Other meaningful iterations included the stereoscope, camera, View-Master (for all of our '80s fans out there) and movie theaters, including 3D and iMax experiences. Joyce explains that all of these iterations have influenced the development of the current virtual reality headset we know of today.

Before moving on to examine patterns, students also consider the benefits and limitations of each of these iterations. For example, a benefit of the stereoscope was that learners in the late 1800s and early 1900s could immerse themselves in a geographical place by looking through dividers. A limitation of that same device is that it depicted only a single image, which was later addressed with the development of the View-Master in the mid-1900s. By considering human needs and meaningful iterations, students can begin to see how each technological advancement has evolved from one innovation to the next. Through this exercise, students explore the benefits and limitations of different iterations and identify patterns of improvement. By recognizing the iterative nature of innovation, students develop a mindset that embraces experimentation, improvement, and the collective contributions of individuals over time.

Once knowledge is captured, the class now starts identifying patterns. Joyce explains "I tell my students, look for the patterns. When you find patterns, you can automate it. That's where formulas come from. Patterns create algorithms." She talks with her students about how, by using this information, humans can also now generate customs and create rules for society. To further illustrate this point, Joyce shares some of the patterns she and her students have uncovered over time:

◆ If it can be automated, it's going to be automated.
◆ If it can be customized, it will become customized.

- ◆ If it can be digitized, it will be digitized.
- ◆ If a tool can be shared, it will be shared.
- ◆ If things can go faster and further or travel faster and further, it will become faster and go further.
- ◆ If we have a tool that can be made to be more sustainable, it will become more sustainable.
- ◆ If it can be documented in some way, shape, or form, it will be documented in some way, shape, or form.
- ◆ If it can free up human time or conserve energy, it will free up human time and conserve energy.

By emphasizing the trends of innovation over time, students can begin to recognize that while specific individuals may contribute to the development of an idea, it is a broader network of human-kind in general, across geographic and generational spectrums, that truly makes innovation possible. She reflects:

> What I have noticed from conversations after presenting on tracing stories of innovation and asking people how it makes them feel is that they feel relevant in the story of innovation. I think people have previously felt overwhelmed and re-placeable. Stories of Innovation show them that actually, no, humans throughout history have been learning how to opti-mize all tools, digital and non-digital, to meet their needs, to enhance their experiences.

Implications for Practice

Joyce's teaching approach exemplifies participatory creativity by actively involving students in exploring and understanding emerging technologies. By focusing on human needs and empa-thy, students develop a deeper understanding of the impact of technology on individuals and society. Navigating fear and ambiguity helps students build resilience and confidence in deal-ing with complex problems. By connecting human needs with emerging technologies, students gain a sense of purpose and realize the potential of technology to address societal challenges. Tracing the story of innovation encourages students to appreciate the iterative nature of progress and recognize the contributions of multiple individuals and generations. Overall, Joyce's teaching approach to participatory creativity empowers students to be critical thinkers, problem-solvers, and active creators in the world of emerging technologies.

The key Implications for participatory creativity in Joyce's picture of practice can be described as follows:

♦ *Tracing the human stories behind innovation*: Joyce emphasizes the importance of uncovering the biographies of ideas and understanding the origins of innovation. By engaging in participatory creativity, students are encouraged to explore the human needs that drive technological advancements and trace the iterative process of innovation. This approach helps students appreciate the collective contributions of individuals over time and recognize the broader network of humankind involved in making innovation possible.

♦ *Emphasizing multicultural and diverse perspectives*: Joyce highlights the significance of considering diverse perspectives and viewpoints in the story of innovation. She advocates for multicultural, multigenerational, ethnic, and gender representations to capture the range of ways that different societies and cultures have met human needs by using available knowledge and resources. By emphasizing diverse perspectives, a participatory approach to creativity prompts students to gain a comprehensive understanding of innovation and encourages inclusive thinking.

♦ *Addressing fear and uncertainty*: Joyce acknowledges the fear and uncertainty that can arise when dealing with emerging technologies. She underscores the need to create a warm and inviting space for students to alleviate their anxieties related to technology. By addressing and minimizing students' fears, a participatory approach to creativity prompts students to move toward their fears with confidence as they navigate ambiguity. Addressing fear and uncertainty promotes an environment where students can explore and uncover complexity in a supportive and empowering manner.

◆ *Supporting empathy and human-centered problem-solving*: Joyce notes the role of empathy in understanding and solving problems related to emerging technologies. She encourages students to find the human element behind the technology and uncover the emotions associated with the problems worth solving. By tapping into shared emotions and experiences, a participatory approach to creativity fosters a deeper understanding of the impact of technology on people's lives and promotes human-centered approaches to problem-solving.

◆ *Identifying patterns and trends in innovation*: Joyce highlights the importance of identifying patterns in the innovation process over time. By recognizing patterns, students can understand how innovation evolves and how it leads to further advancements. A participatory approach to creativity allows students to explore and analyze patterns in innovation, enabling them to make informed decisions as they predict and design future iterations. It also facilitates the automation, customization, digitization, sharing, sustainability, documentation, and conservation aspects of innovation.

Overall, from Joyce's perspective, participatory creativity promotes a holistic and human-centered approach to teaching and learning about innovation. It encourages students to engage with diverse perspectives, understand the origins of ideas, address fears and uncertainties, foster empathy, and identify patterns and trends in the innovation process. By embracing participatory creativity, students develop a mindset that values connection, experimentation, improvement, and the collective contributions of individuals and societies over time.

Fostering Creative Identity Development

Jodie Ricci, a seasoned educator with a diverse teaching background in the arts, has dedicated her over-27-year career to exploring and supporting creative identity development in students. As a former dean of students and chair of performing arts at Hawken School and the new high school principal at Notre Dame-Cathedral Latin School, she has a passion for understanding and nurturing creative growth, which has led her to delve into the concept of participatory creativity.

Meet Jodie

If one entered Jodie Ricci's classroom toward the end of her three-week Creative Process Intensive at Hawken School in Ohio, they might think they accidentally stumbled upon a contemporary art exhibit. Well, either that or a 3M testing facility that allowed only their most colorful and whimsical Post-it Notes. If you met Jodie, you would likely immediately note her humility and gentle nature. When asked about her background and identity, Jodie shared:

> I grew up in a family where I was a first-generation college student. So I think that learning, education, and curiosity have been the driving force of my life. And it has to do with this piece of growing up in, you know, a white, lower middle-class family. And being the first person in my family that was able to go to college has really impacted my work.

It's precisely because of her humility that you would likely never know that Jodie also went on to earn her master's degree in music and certificates in both change leadership and leadership and management and is currently working on a master's degree in educational leadership. You might also not realize just how much time, effort, and energy Jodie has dedicated to learning the art of coaching or how many hours she's spent contemplating "just the right feedback" to convince a struggling student or faculty member that they have something to contribute to creative work.[3] And it is here that our story begins.

Jodie's Context

Jodie's journey with participatory creativity began in 2015 when she transitioned to teaching in the upper school at Hawken School. Troubled by the prevailing notion that some students believed they lacked creativity or were unable to engage intentionally in creative endeavors, Jodie conducted interviews with students across various grade levels and academic interests. This inquiry led her to identify a pressing problem within the community. Jodie explained:

> Through data collection, I identified this problem that I was starting to sense in young people, where several students said that they weren't creative, and they felt they were unable to engage in any form of intentional creativity. And that really bothered me because, we're at a top independent school and students have access to all kinds of experiences and then they're leaving school saying, 'I'm not creative,' or, 'I don't really know how to do that thing that lives down there in the performing arts hallway.'

With her suspicions confirmed, Jodie was immediately inspired to take action, and she began to create a three-week Creative Process Intensive course.

Hawken School is different from a lot of educational institutions in that it allocates the last three weeks of each semester to Intensives for students at both the Hawken Mastery School and the Upper Schools, giving students time to concentrate on a single area of focus all day, every day, for three weeks. According to the Hawken website, Intensives are "immersive learning experiences" intended to "spark deep and meaningful learning that's hard—and sometimes impossible—to inspire in the rhythm and timeframe of a typical class."[4]

As Jodie developed the curricular framework for her own Intensive course, she came across the concept of participatory creativity through research. It was in the pages of the original *Participatory Creativity* book that she found practical guidance and a framework to ground her approach. The notion of reframing creativity as the biography of an idea, rather than an individual's innate ability, resonated deeply with Jodie. She realized that participatory creativity offered a practical path to activate and support creative identity development in her students.

Jodie's Story

Incorporating the theory of participatory creativity into her work, Jodie introduced her students to the concept of biography of an idea. Using the Biodegradable case study from the *Participatory Creativity* text, Jodie emphasized the evolution and contextual nature of creativity, encouraging her students to explore and document the development of their ideas over time.[5] This approach provided a foundation for their final passion projects, where they captured the real-life manifestations of their ideas in action.

Jodie also developed the "SEED Framework," which emerged from and was inspired by observing students' creative processes. This framework integrated four core pathways for students to explore—(1) Social interactions, (2) life Experiences, (3) Environmental influences, and (4) Discoveries—that support the generation and improvement of ideas.[6] By recognizing the importance of social interactions, Jodie encouraged students to understand how their connections with others influenced their creative growth. She explained: "Throughout the [Social interactions] pathway, students engage with others, ask questions, challenge existing assumptions, and grow to understand how different people influence ideas." The framework also highlights the impact of personal identity, past experiences, and the environment on shaping students' creative pursuits.

The SEED Framework serves as one of the core structures of the Creative Process Intensive course. Students are asked to identify a passion project as a catalyst to begin their creative pursuits. "We invite them to develop a passion project over the next three weeks that will help make your place in the world, your small sliver of the world, a little better. We know," she says to her students, "there are so many possibilities. What will your impact be?"

After this initial call to action, Jodie and her co-facilitators (which has included 11 different colleagues over the years) take time getting to know who the students are as learners and individuals. Jodie shared, "One of my favorite questions is 'What is something you want us to know about you?'"

She also highlights the importance of being present, genuinely listening, and asking specific probing questions to help students make their thinking visible.[7]

> For example, a line of questioning might sound something like, 'What are you thinking about for your passion project and why? Why are you passionate about this? What experiences have you had that make you want to develop a project based on this particular idea?'

Through this series of questions, Jodie intends to capture a snapshot of how students' personal experiences influence their own creative process, setting the stage for their continued journey through the SEED Framework. Jodie affirms, "The Experience pathway reminds students that context, point of view, background, and culture influence the development of ideas. It helps them make a connection between identity and creativity."

Then students begin to develop their projects in earnest, collecting and analyzing project documentation and tagging each artifact with an accompanying SEED block (see Figure 4.2).

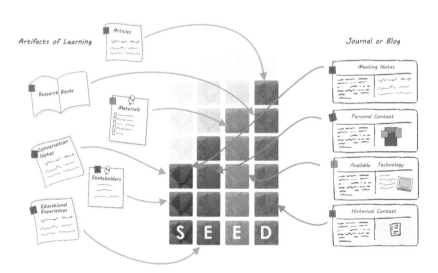

FIGURE 4.2 Young people in Jodie Ricci's Creative Process Intensive course tag artifacts using SEED blocks as they collect documentation.

Image by Jodie Ricci.

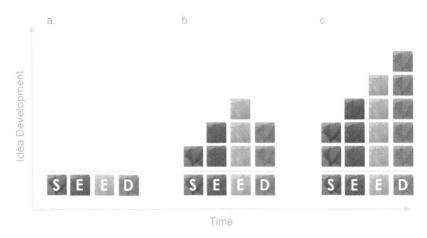

FIGURE 4.3 Young people in Jodie Ricci's Creative Process Intensive course use the SEED Framework to make visible their idea development over time.

Image by Jodie Ricci.

Throughout the project, students make their process visible through documentation, noting areas in need of continued exploration or additional emphasis and, all the while, engaging in discussion with their instructors and with each other. At the end of the project, students create their final SEED graphic documentation and share their process with the class, encouraging further discussion, specific feedback, and suggestions for future action (see Figure 4.3).

While the SEED Framework provides a structured approach to guide students in understanding the multifaceted nature of their creative ideas, it is not the only element Jodie utilizes to support the development of students' creative identities. Jodie's emphasis on task constraints and the acceptance of inspiration from existing works countered the prevailing misconception of originality as the sole measure of creativity.

Asking what other people have done with this particular topic or idea, and also helping students understand that, it's okay to change, hack, and tweak ideas, which we talk about a lot in the course. I think what I was seeing was that students were coming out of experiences in other disciplines where they felt like everything that they had to do had to be original. It had to be something that was brand new that nobody's done before, and they owned this idea.

By inviting representative models from various disciplines to share their creative journeys, Jodie expanded students' perspectives and challenged preconceived notions about creativity.

> And I think that's really helped kids. We brought in a chef to talk about creativity, and they're like, 'Whoa, I never thought about creativity through the lens of food.' Or you know, somebody that works as the chief technology officer for their company and they're like, 'Oh, I never thought that was a creative field.' And with these interactions, students began to see creativity as multiple; a disposition that lives across many different disciplines.

Jodie's dedication to participatory creativity culminated in a powerful story involving her students. Through an activity called *Mount Creativity*, students were asked to name notable figures associated with creativity using the Zoom chat feature.[8] As the chat began to populate, students generated a substantial list, including Einstein, Beethoven, and Tesla. What struck Jodie specifically was the fact that while students could readily identify creative icons, their responses featured only one specific demographic, revealing a lack of diverse perspectives. Jodie decided to probe a little further, asking students what they noticed about the generated list. After substantial thought time and probing, not a single student identified that every name included on their list was an older white male.

What was it that bothered Jodie about this interaction? It was certainly not that Jodie thinks there is anything *wrong* with being a white male. Indeed, she is married to a white male, and one of her children is a white male. What bothered Jodie in this specific instance was that her students, even with prompting, had not yet developed the sensitivity to notice the lack of representation in the list they had generated. Jodie suspected that in addition to accepting a false binary in terms of *what* constitutes creativity, students had somehow internalized a false narrative of *who* represents creativity. She had a hunch that such misconceptions were likely contributing factors in students' reported lack of creative identity.

After this initial formative assessment, Jodie knew it would be important not only to focus on students' creative identity development as individuals but also to ensure she continued to introduce diverse perspectives of not only *what* it meant to be creative but also *who* was considered creative.

> We talk about zooming out and zooming in. The passion project is really about zooming in and thinking about their own identities and how they want to create something that's going to make a difference in the world. But along with that, every day we're engaging and asking them to zoom out and to think about how other people design. And we do that in a variety of different ways. We look at different contemporary artists. El Anatsui is one of my favorite contemporary artists, and there's a great video of his process where he takes bottle caps and all these people come together and start laying down these bottle caps and then he stands back and he takes pictures and then they move them and he takes more pictures.[9]

Jodie explains that through specific questioning techniques, students start to make the connections like "I see this piece in an art museum, but there were all these people that were connected to it. So it just starts to kind of unravel that idea that people create alone."

Jodie goes on to explain the other elements that compose the course.

> We also have them watch episodes of Abstract on Netflix.[10] We tell them to find an episode that interests them and watch that, and then think about the process of this person through this particular lens. They're reading short articles, they're watching videos, they're talking with guest speakers that we bring into the class.

In addition to being exposed to multiple sources of external content, students have the opportunity to participate in creativity challenges.

> We do a daily design challenge in which they have task constraints, and they have to create something, whether individually or collaboratively, and then think about that. They think about what they did in that moment to create this thing. I'm always thinking about how students are interacting with the content. How are they interacting with one another? And then how are they interacting with us?

As Jodie mentioned, one of her primary reasons for creating the course was to support the development of students' creative identities.

> The students are always engaging in reflection and at the end of the course, they do think about their three weeks in the course and their experience and talk about what shifts have happened in their thinking and how their understanding of creativity has evolved or changed.

Jodie shared a few specific student reflections that stood out in her mind. One student noted: "I think rediscovering that everyone is creative in their own way was the most important thing I've learned since I used to think that I wasn't creative. So learning that I'm creative is something I'm happy about." From the perspective of participatory creativity, what this student is expressing is that they have identified how they may participate in creativity in various ways, by playing a variety of different roles.

Expressing how the course opened her eyes to the importance of representation and diverse perspectives, another student shared: "I was not aware of how as a female, my perspective of my world is heavily, heavily influenced by male figures. This course opened my eyes to the importance of representation and diverse perspectives." This epiphany underscored the significance of inclusive and equitable approaches in fostering creative identity development. Jodie felt encouraged that this student was able to uncover some specific influences that may have impacted her own perception of herself as a creative participant.

Jodie's journey as an educator exemplifies the transformative potential of participatory creativity in supporting students' creative identity development. By reframing creativity as a participatory and evolving process, Jodie empowered her students to embrace diverse perspectives, recognize their shared humanity, and challenge traditional notions of creativity. When asked why she does this work, Jodie shared:

> I think creativity is a word that keeps getting thrown around in education. But when you really start asking people, they're lacking strategies and skills for how to do it. And it's very hard work. But really, I think at the end of the day, I believe that we need to do this because I think it creates a more just and equitable society. It allows people to respond to the world that they live in together and to see that the individual really can't do it alone and doesn't do it alone. And that it's so much more beautiful and meaningful when humans try to do something together. And so that idea that everyone is creative in their own way, that they keep saying, I think is what leads me to keep doing this work because I believe they start to really see one another and start to unravel these labels or these systems that say only certain people are invited to this table, and you're not one of them, so go find your identity somewhere else. Quite honestly, we have so many challenges in our world right now, we need people to work together to solve them.

Jodie makes many strong points in her reflection. Perhaps one that stands out is the importance of taking a participatory stance towards creativity to equip young people to address the challenges (and opportunities) that they will face in life and work in the decades ahead.

Implications for Practice

Many implications for practice may be drawn from Jodie's story. Below, we identify the following:

◆ *Addressing students' beliefs about creativity*: Jodie recognized that some students at Hawken School in this particular context believed they lacked creativity or were unable to engage intentionally in creative endeavors. This prompted her to take action and design a Creative Process Intensive course. By incorporating the concept of participatory creativity, she aimed to challenge students' misconceptions about creativity and help them develop a positive creative identity.

◆ *Emphasizing creative identity development*: Jodie's approach focused on supporting students in developing their creative identities. She viewed creativity as a biography of an idea rather than an innate ability. By guiding students to explore and document the development of their ideas over time, she helped them understand that creativity is a dynamic and evolving process. This approach encouraged students to view themselves as participants in creativity with unique perspectives.

◆ *Providing a structured framework*: Jodie developed the SEED Framework, which integrated four core pathways for creative thinkers: Social interactions, life Experiences, Environmental influences, and Discoveries. This framework allowed students to explore different avenues for generating and improving ideas. The SEED Framework provided students with a structured approach to understand the multifaceted nature of the creative ideas they were developing.

◆ *Challenging traditional notions of originality*: Jodie challenged the misconception that originality is the sole measure of creativity. She encouraged students to seek inspiration from existing works and explore how other people have approached similar topics or ideas. By inviting representative models from various disciplines to share their creative journeys, Jodie expanded students' perspectives and helped them recognize that creativity can manifest itself in diverse forms.

◆ *Promoting diversity and inclusion*: Jodie emphasized the importance of diverse perspectives and representation in the creative process. She introduced students to artists, professionals, and guest speakers from various backgrounds to expose them to different fields and cultural perspectives. This approach helped students understand that creativity is not limited to a specific demographic and encouraged them to challenge biases and preconceived notions of creativity.

◆ *Fostering participation and communication*: Throughout the Creative Process Intensive course, Jodie emphasized the value of participation and communication. Students engaged in discussions with their instructors and peers, shared their creative processes, and provided feedback and suggestions for one another. By creating a supportive and inclusive learning environment, Jodie fostered a sense of community and encouraged students to learn from each other's unique perspectives.

Overall, Jodie's story demonstrates the transformative potential of participatory creativity in education. It highlights the importance of reframing creativity, promoting diverse perspectives, and empowering students to recognize their own participation in the creative process. By integrating participatory creativity into their teaching practices, educators can support students in developing their creative identity and profiles of participation, fostering meaningful interactions, and preparing students to navigate an increasingly complex and changing world.

Participatory Creativity in the Culturally Responsive Classroom

Yerko Sepúlveda is a man who wears many, many hats. Currently, Yerko is the Director of Community Engagement and Belonging at the Porter-Gaud School in Charleston, South Carolina.

When we interviewed Yerko for this picture of practice, he was an upper school Spanish teacher at Hawken School in a suburb of Cleveland, Ohio. Also at Hawken School, Yerko has co-taught the Creative Process Intensive course founded by his colleague Jodie Ricci (discussed above in the Fostering Creative Identity Development picture of practice pp. 80–91) and has been a member of the school's Diversity Council. At the time, Yerko was also a Spanish instructor for college students at Texas Tech University in Lubbock, Texas, where he recently completed his doctoral studies. On top of that, Yerko serves as a coach for online courses through the Harvard Graduate School of Education. He is also the father of two young girls.

Meet Yerko

When asked about his identity, Yerko notes that he identifies primarily as an immigrant of Hispanic origin who came to the United States from Chile. He identifies as an immigrant first because, in his words, "Unless you are from the United States, you have never heard the word Hispanic. You realize when you come to the US that you are Hispanic. Before that—you would never assume you are a Hispanic person." So, in order, Yerko identifies as an immigrant male of Hispanic origin and a person of color.

Yerko first came into contact with the concept of participatory creativity informally, as a young person in high school studying theater. He enjoyed acting—and got really good at it—eventually going on to engage in theater throughout his undergraduate studies as he pursued a degree in education. But before his college years, Yerko had a particularly formative experience when he was just about 15 years old. At that time, a local theater troupe in his hometown of La Serena, the capital of the Coquimbo Region in northern Chile, was looking for an actor to play a young character. Yerko joined the group of adult professional theater artists and learned a great deal from their distributed and participatory process. "It was a space in which everyone was working to put together a play," he described, "making costumes, setting up the stage, and giving direction to one another with the final goal of mounting a performance." Naturally, theater is a participatory process, as there are a variety of roles that members of a theatre troupe play onstage, offstage, and behind the scenes. Yerko recalls that the group that he worked with was particularly participatory, as the members of the troupe played multiple roles, and the primary goal of putting together a performance served as the central idea that everyone contributed to as they developed the work over time.

Yerko's next encounter with the concept of creativity, perhaps especially from a participatory perspective, came while he was working as a university administrator. In this position, Yerko had read materials that were shared at a World Economic Forum event, which placed an emphasis on the importance of preparing young people for creative engagement when they joined the workforce. At that time, Yerko made the connection between the need for colleges and universities to equip their students with creative capacities and the demands from the business world for people who could excel at creative work. This connection led Yerko and his colleagues to develop programs to support creative learning experiences for the students they served.

Yerko's "third wave" of creativity encounters came when he began to interact with the work of Project Zero, especially through his role as a faculty member at the Washington International School in Washington, DC. These early interactions with Project Zero led him to Edward's research on the topic and eventually connected Yerko to a broader community of educators interested in supporting more participatory approaches to creativity in their varied teaching and learning environments.

Yerko's Story

Given the many roles that Yerko plays in his professional life, it is not surprising that participatory creativity manifests itself in different ways within the various classrooms he oversees. Speaking of his work as a college instructor, Yerko notes that he incorporates participatory creativity into the semester-long course projects that his students are tasked with, where they must work together to explore a large topic like migration, sustainability, or the role of language and culture in preparing for global readiness. Here, his students are prompted to explore multiple perspectives and to bring in the voices of various stakeholders.

At Hawken School, Yerko implicitly explored participatory creativity with the students in his Spanish classes as they were challenged to work collectively to find solutions to problems or to develop new ideas—all the while increasing their proficiency in the Spanish language. In particular, Yerko tasked his students with studying artifacts—and then developing new, redesigned, or reimagined artifacts together—including images and poems.

Artifacts have played a central role in Yerko's Spanish classrooms, as the exploration of an object through the process of slow looking serves as a trigger for his students to engage in a participatory creative process.[11] In this context, Yerko uses the term *trigger* on purpose—and in a very positive and generative way. "Every time the students interact with an artifact," Yerko says, "the brain will react to it. The artifact *triggers* a response. In a language class, artifacts activate semantic fields and the mental lexicon." Artifacts employed as triggers are meant to activate experiences and emotions and serve as inspiration for invention. When the emotions and past experiences of many students come together, the outcomes are truly works of distributed and participatory creativity.

Through their work as co-instructors of the Creative Process Intensive course, Yerko and his colleagues have been much more explicit about teaching participatory creativity as an approach to distributed idea development. They often began by presenting and problematizing dominant narratives about the creative process that are rooted in individualism. "The way the world tells you to view creativity and how that has informed how you see creativity," Yerko says, "including the hidden messages about who gets to be a creator of ideas and who gets to become a creative icon." The course has then pivoted toward more socially distributed and participatory approaches to what creativity looks like in practice. "Moving away from an *I* perspective, to a *we* perspective of creativity."[12]

Through his work on Hawken School's Diversity Council, Yerko applied the practice of participatory creativity by facilitating the exploration and creation of programming that further developed the school's approach to diversity, equity, inclusion, and justice. Also, as part of the school's in-house training, he led a learning group on intercultural competencies. As part of this learning group, Yerko and his colleagues considered what it means to participate in society and then they considered how to develop strategies to participate in society differently—with the goal of developing intercultural communication practices that are more effective.

Participatory creativity manifests itself differently (and excitingly!) in Yerko's many different teaching and learning environments, but in order to understand what participatory creativity really *looks like in action*, it is helpful to go deeper into specific examples. Below are two such examples from Yerko's Spanish classes at Hawken School.

Using Artifacts to Spur Collective Participation

From the perspective of participatory creativity, *ideas* are the currency of creativity, and *artifacts* are elemental to the development of creative ideas. You may note from earlier discussions in this book that ideas wend their way in the world and take shape over time based on the contributions of various actors. *Products* are the artifacts of ideas. And products can take any number of forms—they may be paintings, sculptures, journal entries, social media posts, mathematical equations, scientific theories, tall skyscrapers, or foam core architectural models. They may also be less tangible things, like subtle utterances and speech acts (i.e., the words and phrases we say or even the sounds we make).

Yerko embraces this broad understanding of what an artifact may be—and gives it a twist. From Yerko's perspective, an artifact can be anything created within a cultural context, but because it is created within such a context, artifacts always bear the imprints of the cultures within which they were created. They are marked, scored, and otherwise stamped by the relationships, beliefs, and practices inherent to their culture (or cultures) of origin.

Within his Spanish language classes at Hawken School, Yerko encourages his students to look closely at tangible artifacts such as images, films, and poems and then to further create tangible artifacts such as images, poems, and essays while creating a little-bit-less-tangible artifacts such as sentences and phrases with the speaker's attitude and meaning (remember, it is a language class after all). All of the artifacts that Yerko's students create—tangible, less tangible, and otherwise—are at the service of supporting greater distributed idea development—within uniquely specific cultural contexts (including the cultures created within Yerko's classrooms).

What might this process of observing, interpreting, and recreating artifacts look like in practice? To begin, Yerko will share a cultural artifact with his students. This may be a song or a work of art or a greeting system or something as simple as a food utensil. The goal here is for his students to extend the artifact by adding to it, to introduce a new perspective to the artifact that it may currently be lacking, to complete a missing piece that is absent, or to create an entirely new artifact inspired by the one the students are exploring.

At the heart of this exercise is the drive to *participate* in the artifact. This is an important (and nuanced) point. Yerko does not want his students to merely engage with the artifacts he presents in his classroom. He does not want his students to merely observe or look (however slowly) at the artifacts under review in his classroom; rather, he wants them to become part of the artifacts' stories. Once again, it is important here to remember that artifacts are the products that shape the greater narrative of creative ideas. By *participating* with the artifacts they are encountering, Yerko's students further contribute to the greater narratives of which the artifacts in his classroom are but one small part. To do this, Yerko has his students consider what might be the *skills* they need to participate with an artifact, what might be the *attitudes* they need to participate with the artifact, and what might be the *behaviors* they need to participate with the artifact. "The skills, attitudes, and behaviors students bring to an artifact contribute to collective participation—and that connects to what the students will do with the artifact," Yerko says. "The goal is to produce a response. And the response is always participatory." He recalls:

As a person from South America, I walk around campus with my *mate*. Mate is a caffeine-rich drink made of *Ilex paraguar-*

iensis leaves, served with hot water and drunk with a metal straw from a gourd. I had noticed that a few of my students looked at me funny, and others directly asked what it was. Therefore, I decided to create an entire unit around it. The overarching goal was how to participate in a cultural practice that is different from your own, and how can we make this cultural practice more inclusive for those from other cultures. We engaged in slow looking to determine the parts, purposes, and complexities of the mate as a system. We also mapped out the system (see Figure 4.4) as we explored the economic, historical, interpersonal, and intrapersonal components of this cultural practice. In the beginning, the students decided they needed respect and openness (attitudes) to explore the unit. They also thought observing, listening, and interpreting (skills) were important to fully unpack this cultural practice. In terms of behaviors, they decided they did not know enough to specify what behaviors they would need. As we engaged in more exploration, discussion, and systems thinking, the students documented other attitudes such as curiosity and discovery. They also realized that analyzing and relating were important skills to add to the match, and

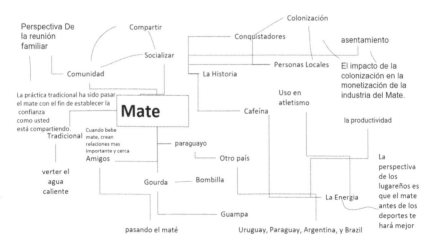

FIGURE 4.4 Mapping artifacts in Yerko Sepúlveda's Spanish classroom. Connections made from the origin points of a single artifact, using language to make connections and develop distributed ideas.

Graphic by Yerko Sepúlveda.

once they had more understanding of the cultural practice, they agreed on understanding other worldviews and socio-linguistic awareness as behaviors necessary to participate in this practice. They also manifested the importance of learning the specific skills/behavior to properly prepare, serve, drink, and pass around the mate. It wasn't until they had fully immersed themselves in this system that they were able to reimagine how to create more inclusive ideas on how to invite others to participate in this cultural practice.

The three-part structure of skills, attitudes, and behaviors is helpful—but it is also important to understand where it comes from. Asked about this, Yerko has a very clear response. The emphasis that Yerko places on skills, attitudes, and behaviors in his Spanish language classrooms comes from the literature on intercultural competence,[13] which further comes from the literature on competence-based learning.[14] "When you talk to people about what you need to be effective in teamwork, especially in diverse spaces," he offers:

> people will tell you 'you need these skills, you need these attitudes, you need these behaviors.' That's why when I teach I focus my students' explorations on what kinds of skills we need, what kinds of attitudes we need, and what kinds of behaviors we need.

Yerko acknowledges that, for many reasons, the word *competencies* is not always well received in diversity work, primarily because it comes from the business world. "It's about someone in authority deciding whether you are competent or not competent," he warns. So instead, Yerko breaks the concept of competency down to its elemental parts—skills, attitudes, and behaviors—and focuses his attention (and his students' attention) there.

The skills, attitudes, and behaviors structure that Yerko utilizes is a helpful way of thinking about how to engage with an artifact, but it is also a helpful way of thinking about how to more broadly support young people in the participatory creativity process. At the beginning of an activity, class session, or unit that will involve creative work, it may be helpful to ask your students:

♦ What are the skills that we will need to engage in this work?
♦ What are the attitudes that we will need to engage in this work?
♦ What are the behaviors that we will need to engage in this work?

Prior to asking these questions, you may further find it useful to co-define this terminology with your students, so they have a clear understanding of what skills, attitudes, and behaviors are. Once you have defined this terminology with your students and generated a list of skills, attitudes, and behaviors for a particular lesson or activity, it may be helpful to keep documentation of these items visible in your classroom, so that you can return to it, and perhaps revise it, regularly.

Finding Your Interests, Tapping Your Network, and Learning Together

One of the requirements that Yerko has in his Spanish classes is that students have to lead a discussion for their classmates. The structure that Yerko has set up is that students have to offer a ten-minute discussion in Spanish about a topic that they are personally interested in and then lead the class in a learning experience that they have designed on the topic. As students begin to develop their presentations and learning experiences, they pursue a combination of individual and collective work, scaffolded by occasional one-on-one coaching sessions with Yerko.

Yerko notes that his students sometimes feel anxiety when they engage in this work, because they are so accustomed to being told what to do, as opposed to identifying their own interests and leading their own learning. Oftentimes, students initially fumble over this task, not necessarily with the learning design element but with the more basic ask to identify a topic that they find personally interesting or meaningful. "When students first propose their ideas about their learning experiences to me, they often talk about paella in Spain or the tango in Argentina," Yerko shares. "I ask them, 'Is this what you are really interested in?' They usually say no, but they assume that the topic they choose has to be culturally informed and pertinent to a Hispanic context." At this point, Yerko redirects his students to probe their own interests. "I tell them to identify their own passions, to think about what has informed them and made them who they are," he says, "and then go out and talk to people." Taking note from their teacher, the students do exactly that: they consider their own passions and then talk to people.

The talking-to-people aspect of this lesson is particularly pertinent to the process of distributed idea development. Once they have truly identified something that they are interested in, Yerko's students talk to their classmates, their family members, their community members, their coaches, other teachers, or people who work in the field of their interests about the topic they would like to discuss. Beyond talking to people, Yerko's students have gleaned information about their topic in many other ways, such as searching the Internet and watching TED Talks—or even issuing surveys about the topic to their peers. Through this process, they gain more and more perspectives on the matter. At this point, Yerko's students have amassed information from a variety of sources—and from a variety of perspectives. Yerko coaches his students through the process of synthesizing all of the information they have gathered by looking for patterns and connecting the dots. Before long, this task becomes less about what a student wants to say about a given topic and more about what the information the student has gathered on that topic has to say about that topic. Yerko refers to all of the information that students have gathered as *data points*. "Once they have all the data points on the table," he says, "we consider what all of the data points are saying individually on their own, consider what the interactions are between data points, and try to figure out what they want to become."

While this could be messy work, Yerko has established a helpful structure. He asks his students to consider three things: *words*, *stances*, and *experiences*. To begin, Yerko asks his students to pay attention to *words*—and to see if there are any words that are frequently repeated. Next, Yerko asks his students to consider the *stances* that are being expressed in the data. In other words, what perspectives are coming to the surface, how are particular perceptions of the topic being expressed, and what are the similarities and differences between the various perspectives and perceptions in the data? Last, Yerko asks his students to consider the *experiences* that are being expressed in the data. In other words, in what ways have different people experienced the topic at hand? When these three elements come together, Yerko's students are faced with the task of considering how particular words are connected to certain stances and how different experiences have informed the stances that various people have toward a given topic (see Figure 4.5). "At this point I ask the students, 'What are we seeing here? What are the data points telling us?'" Yerko shares, "and that's when we create the map."

Except—it's not always a map. Following this information and data analysis activity, Yerko encourages his students to make sense of the information they have gathered by organizing it in a way that makes the most sense to them. Sometimes that is a mind map, but sometimes this organization process takes the form of a drawing, a written narrative, or a Google Doc. "How students organize their data points does not always make sense to me," Yerko says, "but when they flesh things out and present their understandings later on, then it all comes together."

While students are making sense of the information they have collected on the topic they have selected, they are also developing a learning experience for their classmates. This, too, becomes a distributed and a participatory process. Once again, students reach out to family, coaches, other teachers, and discipline-specific professionals for advice. Yerko has found that some of the best learning experiences arise when students tap their own classmates for ideas about how to design an exercise or activity based on their topic of interest.

Asked to expand on a particular example from his classroom, Yerko recalls a story about a student named Monica, who initially expressed interest in the 2019 film the *Joker* starring Joaquin

FIGURE 4.5 Yerko and his students sit down together to make sense of the various data points they have collected to see what they want to become. Throughout this process, Yerko and his students focus on experiences, words, and stances.

Illustration by Julie Rains.

Phoenix in the title role.[15] Yerko describes Monica's experience in his classroom in this way:

> Monica is very shy, and she volunteered to be the first person to share her work—so that was very brave. In our one-on-one sessions, she started out by asking me, "What do I need to talk about?" And that's when I sent her off into the world and told her, "Well, you need to explore the different pieces, the different parts of who you are and how you participate in society and then think about what ideas you want to explore in your world." A couple of weeks later, she met up with me again, and she really wanted to talk about the *Joker* movie and how characters struggling with mental health issues are portrayed in films. That's when I started the process of saying, "Well you really need to talk to more people, you need to bring in your own experiences, you need to go and find out what's the school perception, maybe talk to the school psychologist…," and she started creating this network of people she'd talked to, she started gathering information and bringing in her own experiences. Then a few weeks later, she was brave enough to tell me that she suffers from mental health issues. "Professor Yerko," she said, "this is the reason why I want to talk about this—and I want to have a voice and put it out there." Then we talked about what it means to expose yourself. That's how the process evolved. I was very careful not to push her too much, just let her flesh out her own process. And then she created this awesome experience in class! She was inspired by some of the work we did looking at artifacts, so she put up a picture of a woman sitting on a couch, palm to sunken chest, eyes and mouth open, and got everybody to respond to the picture. She analyzed the assumptions that people were making based on the image they were seeing (most students in the class assumed she was anxious or panicked). Then she facilitated a discussion, and the class ultimately came up with solutions for possible ideas to raise awareness within our own community. So, what started with "I really like the *Joker* movie" went into this space of agentic behavior that warms my heart. It was such an amazing project—and so well informed.

Monica's story—and the opportunity Yerko sets up for his students to explore their own interests and then design a learning experience for their classmates—includes many connections to participatory creativity. In a nutshell, it requires that students probe their own perspectives around a given topic, seek the perspectives of others, synthesize these various points of view, and then bring their classmates into the topic by facilitating an activity. The process is distributed by nature but also geared toward exploring greater complexity around a given topic. As Monica's story illustrates, what began with an interest in a popular movie soon turned into a deep and informed exploration of mental health issues both on a local level and more broadly. It also shows how participating in creativity can be empowering. In this case, Monica shifted her position within the greater narrative of mental health by changing her role from a patient of mental health to someone who was an authority on the matter and an advocate for mental health awareness in her community.

Implications for Practice

The work that Yerko has done in his various classroom spaces connects to the concept of participatory creativity in many ways. Yerko engages his students in the experience of socially distributed idea development, even when they appear to be working on their own. Students are always probing their own perspectives but also collecting and considering the perspectives of others as they solve problems, develop new artifacts, or design learning experiences for their classmates. Through their various projects, Yerko's students are consistently asked to synthesize various perspectives and points of view, including their own. While engaging in this work, Yerko's students implicitly consider—and construct—the biography of ideas as they make connections between different perspectives and perceptions, explore artifacts, and add the next chapter to ongoing narratives.

One of the richest connections between Yerko's work and the theory of participatory creativity is in the way that he uses artifacts in his classrooms. Here, artifacts function as parts of the broader stories they tell about larger ideas. By having them study artifacts—and then make new ones—Yerko invites his students into those narratives and gives them agency in that space. Understanding the imprint of culture on a particular artifact is always a focal point of this work. As they redesign or create artifacts anew, students are cognizant of the cultural meaning they bring to their work—a cultural meaning that comes from their individual perspectives, background experiences, and their own family and community traditions.

Whether he is working with his teacher colleagues or his students, considering the roles that we all play in society is a constant theme in Yerko's work as well. As Yerko's students and colleagues investigate the various social systems they participate in, they consider the ways in which they participate in those systems—and envision ways in which they may participate in those systems differently to bring about more just, favorable, and interculturally conscious outcomes.

There are many implications for practice laden in Yerko's story. Indeed, there are the two activities that were shared here— examining artifacts and developing a presentation and learning experience for one's classmates—but there are also the two strategies that Yerko shared: considering the *skills*, *attitudes*, and *behaviors* necessary to engage in creative work and making sense of a mass of culturally rich data by considering the connections between the *words*, *stances*, and *experiences* that the data has to share.

Identifying Roles for Oneself and Others

With the inspiration of friend and colleague Matt Littell, Erik Lindemann, a third-grade teacher at Osborne Elementary School in Sewickley, Pennsylvania, implemented participatory creativity in his classroom through a project centered on the legacy of Roberto Clemente, one of the best baseball players of all time. Inspired by the concept of innovation and the idea of people contributing to something greater, Erik sought to explore how individuals can impact a person's capacity to innovate. He wanted his students to understand the connection between input, output, and the evolution of greatness.

Meet Erik and Matt

In education, having a thought partner, a trusted colleague who can challenge, connect, or extend one's thinking, is crucial. Or at least that's clearly what both Erik Lindemann and Matt Littell, two inspiring educators in Sewickley, Pennsylvania, think. Matt shared:

> Modeling is a powerful way to demonstrate the power of participatory creativity. I purposefully describe the people and participation that has created the projects and lessons my students engage in. When students see that this is not my idea or creation, but the addition of thinking from our school librarian, a teacher down the hall, last year's students, a teacher across the country, and a research article I read, they begin to embrace the mindset themselves. This impacts my instruction as I then produce higher quality learning opportunities through the participation in my teaching I seek from others.

Erik credits the strong network of Project Zero educators he's encountered over the years, including the "Coaster Club," a group of teachers who meet regularly at Project Zero conferences and institutes to generate ideas on coasters; local school visits, often facilitated by Jeff Evancho; and the Project Zero online coaching community, including participants who continue to enhance the ideation process. He explained, "That network is essential for deep thinking and zooming out to the big rocks we share that guide us."

Both Matt and Erik work for Quaker Valley School District, a small suburban public school district with about 1,800 students situated in Southwestern Pennsylvania. Close to Pittsburgh, Quaker Valley benefits from the city's rich history of innovation and making. Influenced by the Industrial Revolution and its proximity to waterways, Pittsburgh is known for its steel bridges. With the support of influential families and organizations, Pittsburgh and its surrounding school districts have been early adopters of the Maker Movement, establishing makerspaces well before a majority of the country. Correspondingly,

Pittsburgh teachers and learners have shown great interest and demonstrated early capacity for engaging in creative teaching and learning practices.

Erik first heard about the concept of participatory creativity at one of the Project Zero Classroom Summer Institutes. However, it wasn't until a follow-up conversation with Matt, a high school physics and biology teacher at Quaker Valley High School, that he began to consider how participatory creativity might look and sound in his own classroom context. Their initial discussion began in an Uber during the Project Zero Classroom Summer Institute in the midst of deep thinking with others. Erik explained:

> Matt had already been a few steps down the path in terms of articulating what it looks like for his students. And so where I had spent a lot more time with thinking routines, he had spent a little more time on the maker end of things in terms of how he documents the process points. And I was very interested in making that possible and transferring that to what it looks like in the elementary classroom. But it wasn't until we just sat and talked about what it could be until it really was distilled to the point where I could make it turn into something more articulated for the kids.

As Erik mentioned, Matt had developed a keen interest in what maker-centered learning and creativity might look like in his high school science setting. He recognized the importance of ensuring that all students could find their voice and strengths within his class, especially as he noticed some students' hesitancy to participate in science labs. Matt explained:

> Participatory creativity is important because it is an effective way to ensure equity. Students that may have not seen an opening to contribute in the past start to find their voice and their worth to the collective creativity that is happening. They also begin to feel an obligation to the team because they bring ideas and skills that no one else may possess in the same unique combination. Once a student can notice and

name their roles and skills, their confidence builds. Armed with an arsenal of "my strengths," students who may have been traditionally left out of high-quality learning experiences now have the agency to be included and take an Integral role in the collective creation/learning.

Erik and Matt's Story

Inspired by both research and support from Matt, Erik decided to approach his teaching practice through the lens of participatory creativity. He shared:

> I think the first step was during a project to try to find a way to document or report particular behaviors in how we contribute. So at first I put up the generative question, 'How are we contributing?' not only to talk about as citizens, but also to talk about how students were contributing toward something.

Erik introduced the idea of input and output, drawing inspiration from global thinking and dynamic systems. He explained that a person's biography consists of various elements such as people, places, experiences, and ways of handling things, which contribute to their growth. These inputs ultimately shape the character traits and capabilities of individuals, leading to their innovative output. In order to make this concept tangible, Erik decided to create a hands-on experience for his students (see Figure 4.6).

> It's a connection between not only what people are doing to contribute to innovation but also 'How did people get the capacity to innovate?' And in order to do that, to untangle it a little bit, we wanted to create an experience where we were going to build something together.

Erik wanted to choose a topic that was both relevant and of interest to his third-grade students. Bridges in the city of Pittsburgh are symbols of its rich history of building with steel, and Roberto

Name _____   Legacy Investigation Focus: _____

Essential Questions: *How do we contribute?* How do we become capable of making a difference? What character traits are important? What types of contributions do people make? How do contributions to innovations change the world? What parts of the story might be missing?

INPUT - How does _____ become capable of making a difference in the world?

Influences (key events, important people...) When does it happen?	Explain impact of this influence: How does it shape the person's *character traits or interests?*	What does this make us wonder? What questions do we have from looking closely at this input? Who or what might be missing from this?

FIGURE 4.6 A tool that Erik Lindemann developed to help students understand the inputs and outputs of creative idea development.

Image by Erik Lindemann.

Essential Questions: *How do we contribute?* How do we become capable of making a difference? What character traits are important? What types of contributions do people make? How do contributions to innovations change the world? What parts of the story might be missing?

OUTPUT - How does _____ make difference in the world? What area of innovation is this? _____

What contribution does this person make to a type of innovation? When does it happen?	Explain impact of this contribution: How does it shape a type of innovation? What impact does this have on the world?	What does this make us wonder? What questions do we have from looking closely at this output? Who or what might be missing from this?

FIGURE 4.6 (Continued)

Clemente, who was right fielder for the Pittsburgh Pirates, is a revered icon, so Erik chose him as a case study and utilized the metaphor of a bridge to represent his legacy (see Figure 4.7). The class embarked on a bridge-building activity using materials like small bricks and wooden pieces, symbolizing the different components of Clemente's journey. This construction process allowed the students to reflect on the dynamic nature of building something significant and its connection to an individual's legacy.

Throughout the project, Erik emphasized the importance of participation and documented the students' behaviors and contributions. He provided the class with a list of behaviors to observe and record on a clipboard. Erik explained:

> It all started with just giving them the list, letting them decide what they're noticing, talking about the importance of it, and then connecting it back into the instruction and the concept of what it means to develop a legacy. Matt and I talked about the list of roles, and then it morphed over time as to what kids understood and how to continue the conversation.

The students took turns acting as "documentarians" and jotted down the behaviors they noticed within their groups. This documentation served as a reflection tool, that Erik called the "Participatory Inventory" tool. This tool enabled students to evaluate their own contributions and understand the impact of their actions on the collective outcome (see Figure 4.8). The Participatory Inventory tool later became the "Participation Tracker" tool that is featured in the tool kit section of this book (see pp. 199–202).

Erik encouraged ongoing discussions and reflections during the project, acknowledging that not all students would grasp the concept simultaneously. He facilitated conversations within each group, reviewing their documentation and exploring how different behaviors influenced their decision-making process. The students were encouraged to share ideas, discuss their individual

Physical Bridge Structures & Properties	Physical Bridge Functions for this Structure	Figurative Connections to parts of Roberto Clemente's Legacy
1. Tower *Strong, **stable**, tall, massive, huge, metal* *Reaching high; Lights on top*	*Holds up all the cables: lifting the other structures up*	
2. Base (of Tower) *Sturdy, concrete and metal, wide like roots of a tree*	*Goes deep into the earth under the water and holds up the tower; Connected to the tower*	
3. Top Big Cables & Vertical Cables *Strong, flexible (bendy), metal string woven together* *Tied together*	*Hold up the road* *Connect to the towers and anchors*	
4. Anchors *VERY heavy and dug into the ground; Concrete and metal*	*Stretch the cables from one side to the other;* *Keep it from falling over*	
5. Road *Flat with guiderails- can walk or drive on it (can be more than a mile)* *High up*	*Helps vehicles/people get across the big space/water*	

Name _____
Name _____

FIGURE 4.7 A tool developed by Erik Lindemann to help his students use the metaphor of a steel bridge to explore the legacy of Roberto Clemente.

Image by Erik Lindemann.

Participatory Inventory

Group: _____   Name: _____

Roles							
Experimenter							
Project Manager							
Cardboard Tech							
Listener							
Planner							
Connector							
Questioner							
Researcher							
Helper							
Observer							
New Roles							
Total Tallies							

*Which roles do you think you may have played the most? What makes you say that?

FIGURE 4.8 The "Participatory Inventory" tool developed by Erik Lindemann to support his students in understanding what roles they played as they engaged in the process of socially distributed idea development.

Image by Erik Lindemann.

roles, and understand how their contributions shaped the over-all outcome (see Figure 4.9). Erik reflected:

> We came up with terms like 'hogging it' and 'dogging it' and they were using that really well and not in an offensive way to each other, but just like, 'Hey, I'm sorry I was dogging it.' Or 'I'm sorry, I need to stop hogging it.' Or you can say, 'I feel like you're kind of hogging it 'cause I haven't had to say anything.' So those conversations became part of it as opposed to me saying that the kids would be more comfortable talking about that. It's pretty real for all levels of group activity.

By engaging in this project, the students actively participated in the process of building something together, mirroring the concept of innovation and participation. The hands-on nature of the activities, coupled with the ongoing conversations and reflections, helped the students internalize the idea of participatory creativity. Erik explained:

> It was a bit of a pause and reflect on the process of building something together. And it was a way to make it hands-on to understand that, to help build something or even a legacy. It's not just done, it has to happen as a process. And who were the people making it happen? So they were enacting the concept that we wanted to try to help them understand (See Figure 4.10).

Erik's Roberto Clemente project exemplifies how participatory creativity can be integrated into the elementary classroom. By connecting a real-world example to a metaphorical representation, the students were able to grasp the complexities of individual contributions and their impact on collective outcomes. Through documentation and reflection, Erik fostered a sense of agency and encouraged students to think critically about their roles within a group. This project not only deepened their understanding of innovation but also developed their collaborative skills and appreciation for the diverse contributions that shape a person's legacy.

Reflect upon HOW your team built your structure.

1. What behaviors did you notice? How were these helpful?

Behavior	How it helped the team

2. What surprised you about the process of building the structure together?

3. Thinking about Roberto Clemente's Legacy (INPUT/OUTPUT): How does it connect with HOW our teams built the structures?

_____

_____

_____

_____

FIGURE 4.9 A reflection tool created by Erik Lindemann to help his students consider how their behaviors supported the work of their teams during the creative idea development process.

Image by Erik Lindemann.

FIGURE 4.10 The Roberto Clemente bridge-building project was a participatory experience for Erik's students, but it was also a participatory experience for Erik and several others involved.

Illustration by Julie Rains.

Implications for Practice

The work that Erik has done with his students to support their understanding of the participatory nature of creativity is rich with implications for practice. Below we share a few.

◆ *Thought partnership*: This picture of practice highlights the importance of having a thought partner, a trusted colleague who can challenge, connect, or extend one's thinking. Erik and Matt served as thought partners for each other, exchanging ideas and experiences related to participatory creativity in education. Having a thought partner can support professional growth and help educators articulate and implement innovative practices.

◆ *Transfer of ideas*: Erik and Matt's story demonstrates the power of transferring ideas between educators working in different grade levels and subjects. Erik, an elementary school teacher, drew inspiration from Matt, a high school teacher, who had already been exploring participatory creativity in his own classroom. This transfer of ideas allowed Erik to adapt and apply the concept to his elementary classroom context.

◆ *Hands-on experiences*: Erik recognized the value of hands-on experiences in facilitating participatory creativity. By engaging his students in a bridge-building activity that symbolized Roberto Clemente's legacy, Erik created a tangible and participatory learning experience. Hands-on activities can enhance student engagement, understanding, and application of concepts.

◆ *Documentation and reflection*: Erik emphasized the importance of documentation and reflection as tools for fostering participatory creativity. By providing his students with a list of behaviors to observe and record, Erik encouraged them to reflect on their contributions and understand the impact of their actions on the collective outcome. Documentation and reflection promote metacognition, self-assessment, and deeper understanding of one's role within a group.

◆ *Ongoing discussions and reflections*: Erik facilitated ongoing discussions and reflections throughout the project, acknowledging that students may grasp concepts at different times. By reviewing documentation and exploring how different behaviors influenced decision-making processes, Erik encouraged students to share ideas, discuss their roles, and understand the collaborative nature of contribution. Ongoing discussions and reflections promote critical thinking, communication skills, and a sense of agency within a group.

◆ *Integration of real-world examples*: Erik's project with Roberto Clemente as a case study exemplifies the integration of real-world examples into the classroom. By connecting a relevant and interesting topic to a metaphorical representation (bridges), Erik helped his students grasp the complexities of individual contributions and their impact on collective outcomes. Real-world examples enhance relevance, engagement, and application of concepts.

◆ *Participatory skills and appreciation for contributions*: Through the bridge-building project, students developed participatory skills and gained an appreciation for the diverse contributions that shape a person's legacy. By working together, reflecting on their roles, and discussing their behaviors, students learned to value and respect each other's contributions. Participatory creativity fosters engagement, teamwork, and an understanding of the collective nature of innovation.

◆ *Influence of outside actors*: This picture of practice also highlights the influence of outside actors, such as Matt and the Coaster Club, on the development of an idea. Matt's initial insights and ongoing support played a crucial role in Erik's exploration and implementation of participatory creativity. The involvement of outside actors can bring fresh perspectives, support idea generation, and contribute to the success of innovative practices in education.

How Did We Participate Today?

Lee Howard embraces participatory creativity in his classroom to make a positive impact on young minds and foster curiosity and a love for learning. Through the Establishing Communities of Curiosity and Creative Participation initiative, he implemented the Participation Tracker, a versatile tool that allows students to observe and assess their peers' contributions in real-time. Lee emphasizes the importance of understanding the dynamic nature of participatory creativity, encouraging students to explore different roles and gain diverse experiences. By promoting active engagement and self-reflection, Lee creates a collaborative learning environment where students recognize and leverage their participatory roles in various scenarios.

Meet Lee

Lee Howard, a dedicated year five teacher at Bialik College in Melbourne, Australia, embodies the spirit of participatory creativity in his classroom. Inspired by a teacher from his own childhood who fostered a lively and engaging environment, Lee recognized the transformative power of education and decided to embark on a teaching career. He firmly believes that the true essence of education lies in making a positive impact on young minds and kindling their curiosity and love for learning.

In his pursuit of nurturing curiosity and creativity, Lee actively participated in the Establishing Communities of Curiosity and Creative Participation initiative, an exploration of participatory creativity across multiple grade levels. This experience led him to experiment with various approaches to practice, but it was the concept of participation that captivated him the most. Lee's guiding question for this project focused on reigniting students' initial curiosity while navigating the challenging realm of mathematics in middle school. As part of his exploration of participatory creativity, Lee delved into developing students' profiles of participation, seeking to make these profiles visible across all subjects.

Lee's Context

At the time that this work was conducted, Lee was an educator at Bialik College, a Jewish day school located in the suburbs of Melbourne, Australia. In the words of the school's principal, Jeremy Stowe-Lindner, "Bialik is unique as Australia's only pluralistic Jewish school embracing the entire Jewish community regardless of affiliation or practice."[16] With a deep commitment to lifelong learning, Bialik College serves young people from as early as three months old through year 12 in their senior school.

Bialik College has a long history of exploring Project Zero ideas. For over a decade, Bialik College worked with Ron Ritchhart and his colleagues on the "Cultures of Thinking" project, their early learning center is inspired by the work of Reggio Emilia, and, as noted above, for a few years teachers at Bialik College worked with Edward on the Establishing Communities of Curiosity and Creative Participation project.

Lee's Story

To bring awareness to participatory patterns, Lee introduced a powerful tool known as the Participation Tracker (see pp. 199–202) in his year five class. This tool, originally presented as an analytical table in the original *Participatory Creativity* book, was adapted and refined by teachers like Erik Lindemann (referenced earlier in this chapter). Lee observed Erik's implementation and decided to incorporate it into his own classroom practice.

The process of using the Participation Tracker is straightforward. It begins with a table featuring student names across the top row and a list of potential participation roles in the left column. This versatile tool can be employed in real-time observation by an educator, self-assessment by individual students, or peer assessment, allowing students to take note of their peers' contributions. A tick mark goes into a box under a student's name each time they participate in a particular way. As the tick marks accumulate in different boxes, a student's profile of participation comes into view. The roles listed in the tool emerge organically based on student engagement, but Lee chose to use the 13 roles outlined in *Participatory Creativity*.

Lee encouraged his students to work in small groups and after they engaged in a distributed learning experience, asked them to observe and identify the participation roles that their team members played. Notably, he implemented a rule prohibiting students from including their own names in the table, emphasizing that self-perception often differs from how others perceive us. This approach enabled students to track and assess their peers' participation, fostering qualitative and quantitative peer-assessment practices. Lee emphasized that, while the numbers of tick marks in each box indicated the range of roles played during specific lessons over six months, they did not reflect the depth or quality of participation. Nevertheless, students found value in the process, as it allowed them to recognize and name the participatory roles they could embody in collaborative endeavors.

Lee emphasized the need to avoid misconstruing the numbers. Merely having a higher number did not necessarily indicate better or more significant participation than having a lower number. Lee encouraged students to reflect on their participation, irrespective of the numerical value, and consider why certain numbers were higher or lower. He prompted them to consider variables that influenced their participation and encouraged them to give voice to others when they had higher numbers. Lee highlighted that lower numbers could indicate a concentrated and essential focus on specific roles, leading to a greater depth of participation. Reflecting on the information received from peers demanded contextualization and prompted meaningful introspection for both students and their teacher.

Implications for Practice

Lee discovered that student participation varied across different learning experiences, underscoring the dynamic nature of participatory creativity. By analyzing multiple group scenarios, Lee observed that students assumed different roles depending on the content, task, and group dynamics. He posed critical questions about the necessity for students to venture beyond their comfort zones and develop confidence in exploring other participatory creativity roles.

Through his engagement with the Establishing Communities of Curiosity and Creative Participation initiative, Lee recognized the importance of providing students with diverse experiences in the classroom. He emphasized the significance of understanding the dynamics at play and allowing students to assume different roles in various scenarios. The use of the Participation Tracker enabled students to identify and name the multitude of roles they played, empowering them to leverage various parts of their identity as they engaged in socially distributed work.

Socially Constructing the Origins of Us

This picture of practice explores the implementation of participatory creativity at Reuther Middle School through the creation of a student-authored magazine called *The Stories of Us*. This project aimed to amplify the voices of students, particularly English language learners (ELLs), and foster a sense of connection, understanding, and inclusivity within the school community. The project also prompted the "Stories of Us" tool presented later in this book (see pp. 176–179). Rachel Mainero, a former information literacy specialist and now instructional technology specialist for Rochester Community Schools, played a central role in initiating and guiding this work.

Meet Rachel

Rachel is the type of educator one might want to be when they grow up. Her *Harry Potter* alter ego would most certainly be that of Hermione Granger; indeed, her quiet determination, passion for helping others, and love of learning do seem to echo Miss Granger. Yet all of those qualities are also infused with a little spark of daring (she did go skydiving after all), and it is that willingness to step outside of her comfort zone for the betterment of others that is perhaps her most endearing quality.

Growing up in Oswego, New York and the daughter of two public school teachers, Rachel always wanted to be an educator. She explained the importance of her formative years as a student and how those experiences shaped her current perspective:

> I had opportunities growing up where I could volunteer in our school library. And that was incredible for me. I could skip my study hall hour and check out books to students and help return books or put them on the shelves. And then when I got into high school, the books and stories we were reading helped give me new perspectives about the world, and I was able to see the power storytelling truly has. One reason I'm in this media specialist role now is because I want to help propel that power of storytelling and help get diverse books in

the hands of our students so they can see the world through different perspectives and authors.

In addition to recognizing the importance of stories, Rachel recognized the power of collaborative learning experiences that fostered a sense of shared ownership and creativity. She explained:

> I think the most important thing for me is creating opportunities that help our students reach their full potential. I think we need to focus on designing more personalized learning opportunities meeting our students' needs, but also helping our students understand the complexity of our world, understanding the value and importance of getting to know other people's perspectives and truly listening to those perspectives.

She was particularly inspired by the idea of shifting the narrative from "I" to "us" and highlighting the contributions of multiple voices in the learning process.

> It plays into participatory creativity because we create this opportunity where students get to see and understand diverse perspectives. They get to see that not everyone has to look like them. They get to see that the ideas that people share and the ideas that people believe are important to listen to, and it's important to value and honor the perspectives of others and help include them as we start to create a better world.

Rachel's Context

Rachel's then position as an information literacy specialist at Reuther Middle School, a public school in Rochester Hills, Michigan, allowed her to collaborate with teachers, co-teach lessons, and integrate participatory creativity into the curriculum. In April 2019, Rachel enrolled in the National Geographic Educator Certification course, which emphasized bringing an explorer mindset into the classroom and exploring inclusive narratives of migration. Recognizing the opportunity to empower ELL students and challenge stereotypes, Rachel collaborated with the ELL teacher at Reuther Middle School. Together, they developed lessons to help students share their migration stories, foster understanding, and break down biases.

Rachel's Story

The project began as a collaboration between Rachel, the ELL teacher Kendra Seitz, and their students. They provided students with the freedom to choose their preferred storytelling format, such as poems, narratives, or graphic representations. The students shared their migration stories, highlighting the push and pull factors, their personal experiences, and their connections with other students. The classroom became a space where students discovered their shared humanity and built empathy and understanding.

The success of the initial project led to further growth and collaboration. Rachel applied for a grant, which enabled the creation of a student-authored magazine titled *The Stories of Us*. Students from various classrooms, including the ELL students, began working on the magazine. They expanded their focus beyond their individual stories to encompass a broader exploration of migration and the human journey. Rachel explained:

> It started as an ELL project in the classroom, and then it turned into something where I would meet with kids after school, and then we created teacher guides to accompany the magazine. We put a lot of thinking routines in there so teachers could use tools with their students as they read narratives from the magazine.[17]

When students temporarily moved to a distance learning experience online as a result of the COVID-19 pandemic, Rachel continued the meetings. A technology and digital tools connoisseur, Rachel explained:

> We did a lot of this work over Zoom. We found it easiest to start with a digital storyboard to record the ideas for the up-

coming issue. We'd look at the ideas listed on the storyboard and choose a theme. From there, students would determine which stories best fit the theme.

Rachel also shared that the issue topics focused on student interest. "Our second issue focused on India because many students wanted to address the misconceptions people often have about where they were from." Some students also expressed interest in interviewing those close to them to share their stories. Rachel, intentionally shifting her role to that of an equal contributor, explained: "I just let the students go in the way that they felt they were most moved to help create this idea."

It was during the third issue that Rachel mentioned tinkering with a participatory creativity tool. After conversations with Julie, Rachel wanted to try to see if she could help students expand their social circles, seeking the perspectives of more individuals to gather stories for their publication. Rachel and Julie decided to encourage students to not only interview one person to get information but then ask that person to recommend another person, and so on. To get started, Rachel prompted students to think about a specific topic. She explained, "I used a Jamboard for it and put the topic 'migration' at the top and I said, list some people that might offer an interesting insight. Students filled the whole page with sticky notes of ideas."

After that initial brainstorm, students set off to conduct their interviews. They had three weeks to gather information from all of their initial sources and the sources that they, in turn, also recommended. Ultimately, students came back to share their findings, talking about the key themes that appeared in these stories.

Four themes emerged from student interviews:

1. Languages are impacted by migration.
2. Migrant students and families feel that they have challenges they have to overcome.
3. They talked about some of those push and pull factors.
4. Some people were very specific about the places that they had left.

Rachel then asked for volunteers who wanted to turn their interview information into a magazine story. She explained, "I feel like that routine helped structure the way students were extending this work. It helped them to reach out to someone new they hadn't thought of before and add more voices to the publication."

From Rachel's story, it's clear that *The Stories of Us* magazine became a powerful platform for students to share their stories, connect with others, and challenge misconceptions about migration. The project encouraged empathy, understanding, and respect among students and teachers. By publishing the magazine, the students' narratives reached a wider audience within the school community, promoting inclusivity and fostering cultural appreciation.

Implications

Rachel engaged young people in a participatory approach to creativity through her work supporting *The Stories of Us* magazine. Some implications for practice that are drawn from her story are described below.

- ◆ *Diverse perspectives*: By embracing socially constructed idea development, the project encouraged students to go beyond their immediate circles and seek input from a broader community. This approach not only deepened their understanding of migration but also promoted participation, dialogue, and the recognition of the collective nature of knowledge construction. It highlighted the importance of diverse perspectives and the power of distributed idea development in creating a more comprehensive and nuanced understanding of complex topics.

- ◆ *Collective knowledge*: Through this process of reaching out and gathering stories, students were exposed to a diverse range of perspectives and experiences related to migration. Each person recommended by the previous interviewee brought their unique insights and stories to the project, enriching the collective knowledge of the student authors. This approach allowed for a more comprehensive understanding of migration and contributed to the socially constructed development of ideas.

◆ *Co-creation and shared ownership*: By involving multiple individuals in the idea development process, the project fostered a sense of co-creation and shared ownership. The students were not just passive recipients of information; they actively engaged in the process of gathering stories and shaping the narrative of the magazine. This approach empowered students to take ownership of the project and contributed to a sense of collective responsibility for the final outcome.

◆ *Part of a greater story*: By engaging in the *Stories of Us* project and reaching out to so many diverse stakeholders, the students in this project became part of a broader narrative about immigration. They were no longer researching a topic; they were part of that topic. The work of the project—and the stories the students ultimately told—inherently made them part of the greater story.

Rachel's implementation of participatory creativity at Reuther Middle School through *The Stories of Us* magazine showcased the power of participatory learning and inclusive storytelling. The project empowered students, fostered empathy, and created a more inclusive school environment. By amplifying diverse voices, challenging stereotypes, and celebrating shared humanity, Reuther Middle School experienced the transformative potential of participatory creativity.

The Strange Ducks Club—Teaching and Learning (and Other Weird Things that Happen) in a Sandbox

In a 19th-century library with vaulted arches, intricately tiled floors, and elegant brickwork restored to be a vibrant community makerspace, a young girl in a pink shirt with a long braid trailing down her back stands in front of a room of educators. The room is a modern workshop space with a sleek monitor and carefully chosen furniture—it somehow complements the greater space—which is described as a "beautiful ruin." The young woman in the space is Charlotte Own, and the occasion is the 2019 Maker Ed Convening in Pittsburgh, Pennsylvania. Charlotte is a 12-year-old biracial middle school student, living in a medium-sized city just north of Seattle in Washington State. She's also a *strange duck*, but more on that in a minute. Charlotte has flown across the country to be here. Her mom is in the room to cheer her on. And the adult educators in the space are eager to learn from her.

Julie is one such educator, and frankly, she can't help but be impressed by the poise and quiet confidence of this young lady, even before the presentation begins. "You will need your laptop," Charlotte affirms and people nod, booting up their laptops as a few more people mill into the room. The focus of Charlotte's workshop is on her work playing in *sandboxes*—not literal sandboxes full of sand but online environments where multiple users come together to experiment with code and connect over a shared interest. Her goal is not only to introduce these spaces to her adult-educator audience but also to guide them through the process of creating their own.

The type of sandboxes that Charlotte likes to play in are called *fandoms*. Fandoms are a subgroup of Wikipedia. Fandoms, Charlotte describes, "get a lot of people together from all over the Internet to generate a ton of information about a book series, television show, movie, or videogame." As Julie listens to this description, she can't help but make connections to crime-solving dramas on Netflix, where people from across the globe crowdsource information to tackle cold case files or the many fan pages she and her young son have visited in their attempts to tackle *Zelda: Breath of the Wild*, a video game on Nintendo Switch, over the course of the pandemic. Charlotte explains that the fandoms that she participates in are focused mostly on the book series and shows that she enjoys. Although Charlotte is unfamiliar with the concept of participatory creativity in theory, it is evident from her workshop that Charlotte and her online friends have organically gravitated toward the heart of this work.

Charlotte's Story

Fandoms, as we learned from Charlotte, are very participatory places. Within a fandom, there are multiple roles that a user may play—from being a high-level administrator who protects and controls content to a lurker who just takes it all in. They are self-differentiating in that way, making it possible for users to play different roles depending on their level of experience, comfort, and interest in the topic. Fandoms are also further subdivided to support those individuals who want to spend time digging into the direct source material and those who wish to connect and extend beyond it, taking creative liberties to advance the story and choose their own adventure. As Charlotte explains, *canon fandoms* are dedicated to exploring the known content related to a particular topic, and *fanon fandoms* use a topic area as a jumping off point but then allow users to create their own characters, narratives, and interactions. Charlotte has participated in both types of fandoms in a variety of ways, just as students in Julie's former language arts classes have participated in both novel studies and subsequently the creation of their own fan fiction narratives.

Although Charlotte and her friends may not always view them as such, fandoms are effective online learning environments. We may even dare say, classrooms of sorts. They not only support the unique needs, passions, and interests of a variety of learners but also encourage users to learn new information and skills as they need it, and there is an immediate opportunity for relevant application. It is unsurprising then that, as a result of her participation in these fandoms, Charlotte explains she has learned a lot. What she has learned has been not only about content but also about what it means to be a critical reader—and a more conscious reader. Within fandoms about some of her favorite book series, she has met people who are looking for information and who want to talk about a particular book series in a deeper way. It seems Charlotte and her friends have naturally formed the best possible version of online book clubs, leveraging digital tools and technology to transcend the boundaries of the traditional classroom environment. But as a bonus, Charlotte has also learned to code—and how to teach others to code.

While there are multiple entry points to certain fandoms and coding is not always necessary, it is encouraged to make pages more aesthetically pleasing, add content and functionality, and fix bugs and glitches. Charlotte notes that, for that reason, most people who use fandoms want to learn the coding language. And just as virtual learning management systems and Google Workspace have options to promote collaboration, so too does the fandom platform. In fact, as Charlotte explains, the commenting and messaging options were especially helpful in teaching one another how to code. "You saw the code on the fandom pages," she said, "you saw it on people's profile pages, and if you wanted to learn it, then you asked people who were using it if they could teach you." While engaging with the content of a particular fandom, Charlotte also found that fandoms supported "a cycle for users to teach each other the coding language for the site."

Charlotte's experience with fandom sites taught her not only how to code but also a lot about teaching—and that is what her workshop session at the Maker Ed Convening was all about. "As I was teaching, I made a sort of curriculum," she shared. Charlotte's curriculum includes a list of steps to teach others how to code, but there is much more to her approach to teaching than just following these steps. "I also learned how to communicate in an effective way, and what is needed for someone to learn each step." Charlotte describes: "I had to consider how fast to go, how far to go." All of these considerations—and many others—inform Charlotte's curriculum and approach for teaching code.

While she is an astute instructor of code within the fandom universe, Charlotte does not necessarily identify as being an educator. "I'm not a teacher," she said, "but I have definitely learned a lot about communicating information and teaching someone a coding language from scratch." After attending her session and listening to Charlotte explain her fandom process, we would be proud to welcome Charlotte to accept the official title of teacher. Not only is she teaching her friends and peers online the skills and tools they need to participate in her "classroom," she is also teaching educators what school can look like when students have the autonomy and agency to create their own learning environments. While Charlotte may not identify as an educator, what she does identify as is a *strange duck*.

Establishing the Strange Ducks Club

Another important element is the sense of community established by the creators and users of the fandom space. Like many sand-boxes, fandoms have many features. But also like many sand-boxes, fandoms are meant to be tinkered with, and that includes experimentation with their features and functionality. One feature that fandoms have are *clubs*. A fandom club is a place where users who have certain interests can go to discuss a specific topic. Charlotte noted that one of the clubs she was part of was interesting, but it lacked a place to chat. About two years before we had spoken to her (when she was 11 years old), Charlotte said to a friend: "what if we made a club that had a forum where people could chat?" Her friend liked the idea, and together they made the Strange Ducks Club. It was the first forum that users could use to discuss something. But what might people discuss on this forum? Strange ducks, of course!

When we spoke, the Strange Ducks Club was a space where about 200 people went to talk about being weird—and being ducks. "Anyone can join," Charlotte shared, "as long as they are a weird person and like to talk about the weird stuff they did during the day."

Charlotte tells the biography of the Strange Ducks Club idea like this:

> One day I was talking to my friend and I said, "my mom sometimes calls me a strange duck," and my friend said, "I have been called a strange duck, too!" So we made this club, and then our other friend joined and said, "what if we talk about being strange ducks in the club?" And then I was like, "let's make a forum page." So we did. And then a ton of people joined. Once there were a ton of people, we decided that we needed to elect people who would edit the template for the club, add others to the list, and sub-moderate the forum—because it was very active and the administra-

tors were having trouble keeping up with it. So we decided to elect captains. My friend and I are the founders, and we are the ones that elect the captains and make the discussion topics. We also developed a newsletter about being strange

FIGURE 4.11 Charlotte Own and her friend establish the Strange Ducks forum on one of their favorite fandoms, where young people from all over the world can virtually come together to commune about being strange—and being ducks.

Illustration by Julie Rains.

ducks—it's just us writing very random things and putting it on the forum. The captains are the people who keep it alive and keep it running.

Charlotte's experience developing the Strange Ducks Club was an inherently participatory process. Charlotte and her friend initially took inspiration for their club from a club that they had experience with but that lacked the functionality (a chat forum) that they were interested in. The need for the club and a chat forum was prompted by their interest in talking about being strange ducks—which was a playful name that they were each called by their parents. Once the club became popular, there was the need for new roles to be developed to keep the conversation going. Everything about the club can be described as a distributed and participatory process that emerged—and continues to exist—in a social space. Charlotte and her friend have created a safe space for students like them—students who may feel a bit odd or unique and in need of a place to connect with other strange ducks. They have generated a community of inclusive learners all while developing self-sustaining systems and structures to support and maintain a safe and positive online space.

When students and educators step into the realm of online learning, one fear is that of control—that if learners have too much access to chat features and functionality or too much freedom, elements like cyber-bullying or inappropriate posts have the potential to seep into the space. That, of course, is a valid concern and possibility. Charlotte and the Strange Ducks Club, however, are also living proof that young people are capable of developing systems to self-govern and moderate such elements, making it possible to stay connected with their friends online and stay safe at the same time.

Today, there are many clubs on the Internet that are like the one that Charlotte and her friend established not so very long ago. When asked what she has liked most about her experience with the Strange Ducks Club and other fandoms, Charlotte recalls that she learned to code and learned to teach others to code and that she learned a lot about how to quickly form relationships online

—but she highlights the community aspect of fandoms as being what she likes the most. "It's just a great community," she said,

> There is just, like, a community effort to have a good group of people and to have a non-toxic environment—and that is really cool. It's especially cool that the community is made up of kids your own age and it's not, like, adults controlling it.

In a time when interpersonal connection is perhaps more necessary than ever and when in-person hangouts are potentially limited, the importance of online spaces like the Strange Ducks Club cannot be overstated. And that is a big point for Charlotte and her friends: that through the power of their individual and collective agency, they have built a space for themselves to hang out and celebrate the many ways in which they are weird, "which is really fun," she added.

Implications for Practice

Many of the core tenets of participatory creativity are on display throughout Charlotte's tales of teaching and learning in online sandboxes. Perhaps most prevalent among them are the socially distributed nature of idea development and the concept of biography of an idea. That being said, the argument could be made that Charlotte's story also emphasizes the importance of roles within the creative process and—with a little more probing—the profile of participation that is emerging for Charlotte as she engaged in the process of invention and idea development on the various fandoms she's been part of.

There are also many implications for teaching and learning practices that can be drawn from Charlotte's story. Here, we discuss four:

- ◆ *Provide opportunities for young people to connect and learn from others*: Ideas become more nuanced and complex when young people are given the opportunity to think together. Charlotte and the Strange Ducks Club crowdsourced content and ideas not only about their favorite book topics and characters but also about the coding aspects of their fandom. This invited the participation of users who were knowledgeable in computer science and simultaneously of those who were passionate about language arts. Learners like Charlotte and the Strange Ducks Club found many influential collaborators outside the walls of their "creative classroom," encouraging the habits of perspective seeking and information sourcing to represent a variety of viewpoints as part of the ideation process.

◆ *Follow students wherever they lead and help them make connections wherever they go*: Throughout the creative process, learners might extend their thinking beyond the expertise of the educator in the room. It is important for educators to follow students where they lead, to learn with them along the way, and to help make connections to new sources of knowledge and expertise as they continue down the pathway of group discovery. Imagine what would be possible if Charlotte were invited to create and share her "Book Club" fandom at school? Learners would be encouraged to meaningfully participate in authentic discussions about their reading passions and interests while engaging in cross-curricular learning to support coding fluency.

◆ *Creativity is what young people already do, not something new they must become*: Participants enter the creative classroom with a wealth of talents, skills, background experiences, and cultural perspectives. Just as Charlotte and her friends have expertise in the creation and moderation of Wiki Fandoms, so too do their classmates in other areas. What if their learning process in school, rather than relying on contrived learning episodes, were shaped by these foundational understandings and tailored to fit the unique needs of the group? Students could then continue to expand and deepen their existing knowledge base throughout the creative process.

To foster this type of learning, first ask students to share an area of expertise with the class; then invite the class to brainstorm how that passion or interest might connect with the class or discipline. For example, in

Julie's former elementary media classroom, students brainstormed what they loved to do and then chose one focal area. From there, they brainstormed all of the skills they might need to be knowledgeable in that passion area. Then they made connections to the skills they might need to be successful in media class. One student chose cooking as her area of passion, brainstorming that she would need to be organized, pay attention to the steps of a recipe, know how to use the cooking tools, and be imaginative in her exploration of new ingredients. She and her classmates were then able to recognize that she also needed to be organized in media class, pay attention to the way the books were organized, understand the steps and book checkout process, and participate in the creative process to form new understandings.

◆ *Don't forget joy*: It was clear from our conversations with Charlotte that she and her friends were proud of what they had created. Participatory creativity is, by all means, serious business, but such learning experiences can (and should!) also foster the thrill of developing new ideas in the company of others, the pride of understanding how one's individual agency can contribute to a greater goal, and the joy involved in participating in the process of change.

Amplifying all Voices in the Creative Classroom

In this picture of practice, we explore the transformative journey of Erika Lusky, a passionate speech pathologist at Rochester High School in Rochester Community Schools. Erika's dedication to her students and her commitment to fostering their communicative abilities led her to explore innovative approaches to enhance their learning experience. Through the integration of participatory creativity, Erika embarked on a remarkable adventure with her class, resulting in the creation of unique board games that not only facilitated communication but also empowered her students and the adults around them.

Meet Erika

When one meets Erika Lusky for the first time, some things are just readily apparent. Her warm and welcoming demeanor immediately puts people at ease. Intuitively, people know that Erika is someone they can trust. And they're right. Both inside and outside of the educational environment, Erika is described as passionate, positive, outgoing, and caring. She's what Malcom Gladwell might refer to as a "connector," continually linking people and ideas to create the best possible outcomes for all involved.[18] The child of Hungarian Jewish immigrants and the daughter and granddaughter of Holocaust survivors, Erika has grown up a passionate advocate for togetherness and community. Perhaps the idea of participatory creativity resonates well with her as stories of her family's journey remind her of participation. She's also the sort of person who somehow has the ability to plan a Passover family gathering while conducting student planning meetings, teaching lessons in three classes, and planning a building-wide professional development experience (all of which, by the way, will have been executed beautifully). It's no surprise then that Erika has been closely involved in multiple research initiatives at Project Zero, most notably her work with the "Cultures of Thinking" project.[19]

For almost a decade, her innovative and strength-based approach to supporting neurodiverse students in a variety of contexts and settings has enhanced the field of education. Perhaps one of the most important aspects of Erika's work is that of student voice, from both a literal and a figurative perspective. For over 27 years, Erika has supported students as a speech and language pathologist for Rochester Community Schools. She has worked across all grade levels and disciplines and with students with a variety of strengths and ability levels. If you asked her, she would share that "all students have a voice" and she "encourages them to prove it." In her current role as a special education instructional coach for Bloomfield Hills Public Schools, Erika continues to work alongside educators in supporting neurodiverse learners.

Regardless of her title or role, Erika's dedication to her students and her commitment to fostering their communicative abilities continually lead her to explore innovative approaches to enhance learning experiences for all. Through the integration of participatory creativity, Erika embarked on a remarkable adventure in her former role at Rochester High School, resulting in the creation of unique board games that not only facilitated communication but also empowered her students.

Erika's Context

In her role as a speech and language pathologist, Erika felt strongly that, whenever possible, it was best to support students within their naturally occurring environments. Language is a community sport after all, so utilizing authentic, spontaneous opportunities to practice speaking and listening seems only natural. This often meant co-teaching alongside special educators to support them during their language arts classes, and such was the case in Tarra Dodge's self-contained cognitively impaired classroom at Rochester High School.

Within the class, a majority of students were non-verbal and utilized assistive technology, such as iPads with specific core vocabulary, to communicate their needs, wants, interests, and emotions. Part of students' educational programming was to practice leveraging digital tools not only to communicate their needs and preferences but also to socialize. Students would have multiple opportunities in a variety of contexts to practice those daily living skills, including their free choice time on Fridays. Erika noticed that during that time, students would consistently reach for the same pre-chosen, pre-existing board games from the shelf. She began to wonder if there might be a way to reimagine this activity to support the development of student voice. Upon reflection, Erika decided to introduce a novel activity where instead of using pre-made board games, the students would construct their own.

Erika's Story

Erika, filled with excitement and anticipation, presented the idea to her students. Instead of dictating their activities, she wanted to give them the freedom to explore their creativity and tap into their own interests. The students eagerly embraced the opportunity, their faces lighting up with enthusiasm for something new and different. Erika encouraged them to brainstorm and create games they had never played before. One student, Lucy, had a brilliant idea inspired by her teacher's favorite game, Candy Land. She proposed recreating the game as "Dodge Land" and enthusiastically began designing the board. Erika marveled at Lucy's empathy and intuition, as she changed the game's name to honor her beloved teacher, Mrs. Dodge. Lucy's idea sparked the interest of her peers, who flocked to her table to join in the creative process. Erika noticed that the groupings were formed purely based on personal choice and interest, disregarding ability-based groupings and avoiding student labels of any kind. Students went to the stations that resonated with them, embracing the opportunity to participate in creativity.

At Lucy's Candy Land station, the students participated as a collective and worked on bringing their unique vision to life. Lucy meticulously crafted the board while her classmates assisted in creating the game pieces. Using available materials in the classroom, they used different-colored scraps of paper to represent the players. Lucy intuitively understood the need for different colors to distinguish each player, just like in the original Candy Land game. The students designed colorful spots on the board, and the cards they created matched those colors, dictating players' movements. During the building process, Erika supported Lucy and her classmates' language development by prompting them to use their voices, in this case by using iPads with pre-programmed communication boards, to explain what they were doing and why they were doing it. With the support of another educator, Nate, a student with his own iPad, worked on creating phrases to participate in the game. Nate's determination and enthusiasm propelled him to actively engage with the game, joining in and playing alongside his peers. At the same time, Erika encouraged Lucy to continue to explain her thinking beyond "yes" or "no" answers and used a conversational approach by rephrasing and summarizing Lucy's words, fostering a supportive environment for effective communication.

While Lucy's group worked diligently, other students explored various activities, rotating between different stations and games. Each game became a hub of creativity, offering an inclusive space for students to immerse themselves in their creations. As the games progressed, new players joined in, and the games evolved organically.

At a nearby table, Paul, another student in the class, carefully traced a large circle on a posterboard with a black marker. Just as Lucy was inspired to create her game in honor of her favorite teacher Mrs. Dodge, Paul was inspired to create his game after time spent exercising with his dad. Erika noted the role of Ms. Lewis, a paraprofessional, in assisting Paul. She encouraged Paul's independent actions and decisions throughout the game creation process, supporting his voice and vision to the fullest extent possible. In Paul's game, players rolled a "yes or no" to determine if they would move or rest during their turn, resembling moves made at the gym during exercise with his dad. If a player rolled a "yes," they would do the assigned action on their game board space, ranging from the chicken dance, to jumping jacks, to frog jumps. If they rolled a "no," they had a turn to rest. To design the game and choose the actions, Paul communicated using his iPad, selecting words and symbols to express himself. For example, to communicate a "frog jump," Paul chose the "action words" category from his iPad, followed by the word "jump." Ms. Lewis responded by asking, "Jump like what?" and Paul then selected the word "frog" to create the full action needed for that space. Paul and Ms. Lewis took turns in a similar fashion until all of the board actions were complete.

While some students were focused on the creation of the games themselves, still others were focused on enthusiastic participation. Erika explained that the students completely transformed their classroom engagement, expanding their typical classroom participation to reveal more about themselves as thinkers and learners. "I'll never forget how Caleb interacted and engaged in class that week," recalled Erika, "Typically, he selects a rocking chair and prefers to rock for most of the day. But on this day, he went and played every station's game." This engagement equally impacted both the player and the game designer. Erika noted the pride in Paul's face as he watched students play the game he created. "Like I just feel it somewhere. I know this is what he's thinking. He's thinking, 'someone came over after I put all this work into this, and is playing my game.' And I know there's a sense of pride in him right now." Increased engagement and ownership weren't the only byproducts of this experience, however. Leveraging digital technology and student passion made personalized learning possible while incorporating new language and encouraging creative expression.

In still another part of the room, Nate, a student who often faced sleep-related challenges that hindered his participation in school, was dancing to his favorite music artist Justin Bieber. Nate was inspired by GoNoodle, a freely available set of short, interactive videos designed to help students move throughout the day. And during this class, he made his own GoNoodle. Using his iPad, Nate guided others in an interactive dance routine following Justin Bieber's moves, enhancing his personal connection to the activity in the process. To design the game, Nate used his understanding of Google Search on his iPad to find his preferred Bieber song. This opportunity to design his own interactive learning experience shifted Nate's experience in school. Erika explained, "The cool part is, his whole body language changed, you know? From head down sleeping to being active. This is more than like, just go take a walk and come back. Like, that's a break. This was different." By inviting students as active participants in their own learning, Erika, Tarra, Ms. Lewis, and the whole teaching team shifted what it meant to be a learner during free choice time and beyond. Ms. Dodge specifically remarked, "You've shifted the way I view my students."

Erika's exploration of participatory creativity in her classroom led to a profound and transformative experience for her students. By encouraging them to construct their own board games, she fostered passion, personalization, and communication. This journey allowed each student to showcase their unique strengths and contributed to their personal growth. Through participatory creativity, Erika not only facilitated the development of communication skills but also created a classroom environment filled with joy, autonomy, and a sense of accomplishment.

Implications for Practice

Throughout Erika's story, many implications for practice come to the surface, including the following:

- ◆ *Engagement and empowerment*: In Erika and Tarra's classroom, co-designing learning experiences in a participatory fashion played a central role in empowering and engaging students. By encouraging them to construct their own board games, she empowered her students to become active participants in the creative process.

- ◆ *Teacher estimates of achievement*: Educational theorist John Hattie asserts that teacher estimates of achievement have an effect size of 1.30, which is significant in terms of impact.[20] "Teachers with more accurate judgments are more likely to calibrate the optimal difficulty of tasks and be more able to provide stretch feedback." In her design of this experience, Erika accurately gauged students' achievement level and stretched their thinking in new ways.

- ◆ *Independence*: Erika's decision to move away from traditional, pre-existing games and embrace a more open-ended and student-driven approach served as a catalyst for student agency and ownership of the learning process. By allowing her students to express their ideas and preferences, Erika fostered a sense of autonomy and self-directed learning.

- ◆ *Student interest*: Furthermore, Erika's students formed groups based on shared interests and worked together to bring their game ideas to life. This collaborative environment not only enhanced their communication skills but also nurtured a sense of community and peer support.

- ◆ *Leveraging technology as a participant in the creative process*: As they designed their board games, Erika and Tarra's students leaned into technology and other non-human actors as participants in the creative process.

Erika's classroom experience demonstrates that participatory creativity promotes engagement, self-expression, and personal growth. By integrating this approach into her teaching, Erika provided her students with a meaningful and transformative learning experience, enabling them to develop crucial skills and unleash their true potential. By embracing the principles of participatory creativity, Erika and Tarra's classroom became a space where her students could thrive, take ownership of their learning, and build upon their individual strengths.

A Participatory Approach to Assessment

Jeff Evancho, an experienced educator based in Pittsburgh, and Peter Wardrip, a former researcher at the Children's Museum of Pittsburgh and now researcher at the University of Wisconsin-Madison, joined forces to explore and develop the concept of values-based assessment, inviting a participatory approach to assessment in the process. They utilize the Agency *by* Design framework for maker-centered learning, emphasizing the importance of becoming sensitive to core capacities and personal values in the learning process.[21] Through their monthly workshops, they engage a diverse group of educators from various contexts to explore and identify the types of learning they value most. This picture of practice outlines their approach to developing sensitivity, assessing learning, and intentionally designing for dispositions such as curiosity and creativity.

Meet Jeff and Peter

Jeff has worn many hats over the years. He began his career as an art teacher at Carrick High School in Pittsburgh Public Schools and has since served as art teacher, quasi administrator, and Project Zero programming specialist at Quaker Valley School District, assistant superintendent of secondary education at South Fayette School District, and director of partnerships and equity. Though his positions may have evolved over the years, one constant has remained. Jeff is a change-maker. He's the sort of person who can see the possibilities in any situation and then use that sensitivity to take action for good. His efforts have created a thriving network of learners in the surrounding Pittsburgh area, focusing on incorporating Project Zero ideas and philosophies into their educational contexts, and that influence has created ripples that have enhanced the educational opportunities for learners far beyond the Pittsburgh area. At his core, Jeff displays the mindset of participatory creativity. His actions bring people together, and for that reason, it's no surprise that his approach to assessment embodies a participatory creativity perspective.

Peter is a former researcher at the Children's Museum of Pittsburgh and now assistant professor of STEAM education at the University of Wisconsin-Madison. His thoughtful nature and penchant for synthesizing complex ideas are readily apparent, and this skillset enhances the learning experiences for young children and adults alike. Peter brings his extensive knowledge and experience in the science of learning and development as well as adult and professional learning. His gentle disposition and expertise in facilitating meaningful discussions and fostering a culture of curiosity make him a valuable contributor to any team or organization.

The connection between Jeff and Peter emerged from their shared interest in promoting a maker mindset in education. They met in Pittsburgh, where their passion for empowering educators to design and create the conditions for student agency and creative experiences sparked an instant connection. Recognizing their shared vision, they embarked on a journey of research, professional growth, and participatory creativity.

Jeff and Peter's Context

Combining their diverse backgrounds and expertise, Jeff and Peter developed a comprehensive framework for fostering values-based assessment in educational settings. Jeff explained, "Assessment is this ongoing development of understanding of what we hope and desire for our students really rooted in, how do we know that it's happening?" This framework aimed to guide teachers in becoming more sensitive to their values, designing intentional learning experiences, and assessing the impact of their instructional practices. Jeff reflected:

> I think a lot of our work is obviously informed by the Agency *by* Design framework. And the concept of becoming sensi-

tive to something is something that really resonates with everything that we do. So it's not just becoming sensitive to the core capacities to develop agency; we thought a lot about becoming sensitive to the things that we value most. The type of learning which we have come to find is mostly dispositional. So everything that we have built has been built around, 'How do we become sensitive to the things that we care most about to develop a deeper understanding of that? which then helps us identify where that learning exists.'

To tinker with these evolving ideas, Jeff and Peter formed a cohort of diverse educators from different educational contexts in the surrounding Pittsburgh area. Jeff added:

And by diverse we mean the context in which we educate. That learning happens everywhere, and it's really important that we have different types of educators. Traditional classroom teachers from a Kindergarten to Grade 12 spectrum in public schools, independent schools, out of school time… And anybody that works with kids in a learning environment. We want to get them all together to say, 'Okay, what does learning look like?'

Funded by a mini-grant from the Grable Foundation, this cohort would meet monthly to attend workshops, pilot tools and resources, visit one another's educational contexts, and participate in a supportive community of educators dedicated to fostering the development of dispositions they value most. Jeff explains:

Over years we have found that there are certain things that we do with the educators that resonate with them, that holding time to interrogate their artifacts of their practice is something they care deeply about. They care deeply about being validated by other people that are working with kids in similar ways. They care deeply about looking at learning and different contexts. They care deeply about living in the space of developing an understanding for what the learning cares about. And it's not a, Jeff and Peter designed something. We designed things that have been informed by the support and participation of others.

Jeff and Peter's Story

Before we go deep with Jeff and Peter here, we feel it is helpful to clarify what they mean by their use of the word "sensitivity." Sensitivity is one of the three parts of the *triadic theory of dispositions* established by David Perkins, Eileen Jay, Shari Tishman, and their colleagues at Project Zero.[22] Here, a disposition is described as a way of seeing and being in the world. And there are three parts to a disposition: capacity, or the ability to do something; inclination, or the motivation to do something, and; sensitivity, or the alertness to occasion as to when to do that thing. Here, "that thing" would be considered some sort of cognitive ability. Having a *sensitivity to design* features prominently in the Agency *by* Design framework for maker-centered learning. Within this context, having a sensitivity to design means many things, but it mostly means having a heightened awareness to the designed dimensions of one's world and seeing the designed world as malleable. OK, now back to Jeff and Peter.

Jeff and Peter view sensitivity as a form of assessment. Rather than considering assessment as a final test or rubric, they emphasize the continual development of understanding and judgment. Educators start by becoming sensitive to their values and the manifestations of those values in student learning. By examining artifacts and evidence of these dispositions, they deepen their understanding of how they can design for and assess them in their instructional practice.

What did learning in this cohort look and sound like? To begin with, Jeff and Peter invited educators to reflect on what they value most. Inspired by the "Cultures of Thinking" work of Ron Ritchhart and the big rock analogy of Stephen Covey,[23] Jeff and Peter ask educators to consider how they allocate time for what they value most by means of a "Big Rock Routine" (see Figure 4.12). Once educators have established the dispositions or characteristics that are important to them, they form groups with

The **Big Rock** Routine

"It is not, as some students initially suggested, that you can always fit more into your life. Rather, the jar signifies our life, and the big rocks are the things we value and feel are truly important. If we place our big rocks in first, there is space to fit in the other things we have to do."

—Ron Ritchhart
Creating Cultures of Thinking

What do you value?

What makes you say that?

What do you need to prioritize what you value?

What makes you say that?

Purpose: What kind of thinking does this routine encourage?
This routine encourages individuals to synthesize and capture the essence of their own beliefs while connecting and listening to others.

Application: When and Where can it be used?
This routine can be used by teams of leaders, teachers, students, or other community members trying to prioritize time around ideas that matter.

Launch: What are some tips for using this routine?
This routine works well in small groups of 3-5 participants. Each member of the group needs two small objects (e.g., rocks, stones, quarters, blocks, etc.) to represent each of the bolded questions above. One by one, the group members then present their first object, answering the first question and explaining their reasoning. All other members listen attentively until the speaker is finished. Then, they may ask clarifying or probing questions. Once all members have shared, the group members present their second objects, sharing their reasoning. Again, other members listen attentively until the speaker is finished then they may ask clarifying or probing questions.

*Variations might include merging these ideas with either a Chalk Talk Routine (to capture all the ideas in writing) or as a Microlab Protocol (to structure time). If the group wishes, they might connect ideas together to create a team list of priorities for future planning.

FIGURE 4.12 The "Big Rock Routine" developed by Jeff Evancho and Peter Wardrip to ask educators what they value most in their practice.

Design by Julie Rains.

educators of similar interests. Through this affinity clustering, educators with similar values are able to engage in dialogue and explore how to become more sensitive to those values. They use an adapted "Looking at Students' Thinking" protocol to facilitate discussions around artifacts and student work, developing a deeper understanding of how curiosity, playfulness, resilience, or other characteristics manifest in the learning process.[24]

Another tool Jeff and Peter mentioned is the "Looking for Learning in the Wild" template,[25] which serves as a documentation framework for educators to observe and document instances of desired values in various learning environments. Inspired by a keynote presentation from David Perkins, educators walk through different classrooms or learning settings and capture observations of how values such as curiosity manifest in those contexts (see Figure 4.13). Jeff elaborates:

> And when you're walking through that classroom, you might be an elementary school art teacher, and you're going to now walk into a charter school in an urban environment that you've never been in before, and you're going to walk into a math classroom and now you're looking for curiosity. In this completely foreign environment to what you're normally used to and you're documenting, how does it manifest? What are things that you hear? What are things that you see? What are the interactions? What does the environment look like? And you're capturing all of that. And so each educator is doing that based on their value. They're walking through different learning environments and they're documenting where their value is becoming visible to them.

These observations are then shared and discussed within affinity groups, fostering a collective understanding of how values are expressed in different settings.

Once educators have developed a sensitivity to their values, they embark on a design challenge to intentionally incorporate those values into their teaching. Mini-grants are provided to educators to facilitate the design process without constraints. Through this design challenge, they create learning experiences that align with their values, such as fostering curiosity or promoting creativity. This process involves inviting students into the design process, encouraging active participation and collaboration.

Walking through Classrooms

Pre-Observation

In anticipation of your observations, what do you hope to see as evidence of learner engagement in your value?

What value will you be looking for?

What do you hope to see? *What will evidence of engagement in your value look like?*	Why do I say that? *What is it about these examples of engagement that aligns with your value?*

During Observations

	What do I see? *What does it look like for learners to engage in this value?*	Why do I say that? *What is it about these examples of engagement that aligns with your value?*
1		
2		

FIGURE 4.13 The "Walking through Classrooms" tool was designed by Jeff Evancho and Peter Wardrip to support educators in observing pedagogical values in action.

Design by Jeff Evancho and Peter Wardrip.

The design challenge prompts teachers to explore how to foster curiosity and other values within specific topics or subjects. Jeff explains how it works:

> The host school facilitates a design challenge with students [and teachers] and we really push on, "Often you are the designer as a teacher for your kids. What happens when you invite kids into that practice and you say, 'This is what we're designing for, we're designing so that we can be curious about this topic, how might we do it?'" And design challenges are born. And that's another way to think about design challenges that aren't just spaghetti towers. They're intentional designs for things, and we consider who's doing the designing and what they're designing for. And how do we know that it worked? How do we know that it worked, is the assessment piece. So that's one piece that we do to continue to build sensitivity.

Another way Jeff and Peter build sensitivity is by utilizing a "Radar" tool adapted from Luma, a Pittsburgh design thinking firm.[26] This tool helps educators evaluate the ease or difficulty of making learning visible (see Figure 4.14). It allows them to identify elements that are easy to document and assess as well as aspects that require further consideration and development. By using the "Radar" tool, educators can better understand the complexities of their instructional designs and make informed decisions to improve their practice. Jeff highlights the importance of collective participation in the process:

> And we have educators do that with other people. They don't do that as an individual. They may have some moments where they capture their thoughts as an individual, but we're constantly bringing them together in like affinity clusters, where common dispositions are happening.

Throughout this experience, assessment is approached from two perspectives. First, the process of becoming sensitive to values

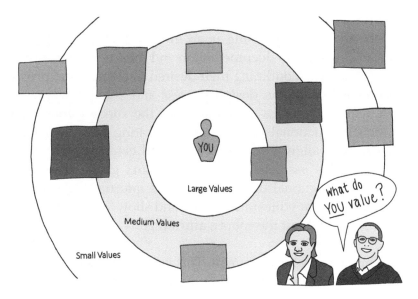

FIGURE 4.14 The values-based assessment "Radar" tool designed by Jeff Evancho and Peter Wardrip to support educators in becoming sensitive to their pedagogical values.

Design by Jeff Evancho and Peter Wardrip.

and developing a deeper understanding of their manifestation serves as a form of assessment. Educators continually assess their growth and understanding along a continuum, refining their judgment and design practices to better support desired outcomes. Jeff explains:

> "I used to think and now I think" is a great tool for assessment.[27] Educators might say, I used to think creativity was this. My students are doing this. Their evidence and their artifacts of creativity are X, Y, and Z. "And I know this is my current understanding of creativity. As I become sensitive to creativity and I go through these experiences, my understanding and my judgment of how it manifests, how I feed it, how it develops, how I design for it, how I formatively am capturing it, how I am summatively capturing it. In the end, that sensitivity on that continuum is grow[ing] and my assessment of what creativity is, where my students need to be on that continuum is evolving."

Assessing the effectiveness of the design challenges and the impact on student learning is an integral part of the process. Educators engage in documentation and reflection. They present value statements, outlining their desired outcomes, and provide documentation of the design process and student work. This documentation serves as evidence of the success and impact of their instructional designs, demonstrating how their teaching practices align with their values and contribute to student learning. This assessment helps educators gauge the success of their instructional designs and make informed adjustments. Jeff explains that educators present and showcase their learning journey throughout the cohort, affirming:

> This is my value statement. This is what I believe I want my students to be. This is what my design process looked like. And here's my documentation of how I know that it worked. And that happens in this final showcase that we do at the end of the year.

Jeff and Peter's dedication and engagement in creativity continue to shape the educational landscape. Their combined efforts, fueled by their passion for supporting the capacity of educators, have made a lasting impact on both teachers and students, helping them unlock their creative potential and cultivate a love for lifelong learning. Jeff reflects:

> I think the entire thing is participatory. I came into the broader story when AbD was working with Oakland to collect things like a sponge to say this is awesome stuff and I wanna be doing some things with folks that I hang out with in Pittsburgh. And, everyone was kind enough to let me hang around. I mean just to see all of these beautiful outgrowths, which are also an outgrowth of what has started in Oakland way back in the day, which came from, other Project Zero projects and informed by them, so there's just this throw a rock in a pond and you see the ripples. We're one of the ripples. So I do think it is a hundred percent participatory, and we would not want to take credit otherwise.

Jeff and Peter's implementation of participatory creativity in their learning environments emphasizes the importance of becoming sensitive to values, intentionally designing for dispositions, and continually assessing the effectiveness of instructional practices. Through their monthly workshops, educators gain a deeper understanding of how to design and assess for values such as curiosity and creativity. Their approach encourages active student involvement, reflection, and participation, ultimately fostering a rich and engaging learning environment.

Implications for Learning

Throughout Jeff and Peter's story many connections to practice can be made. Some implications that educators may consider include the following:

- ◆ *Affinity clustering*: The formation of groups with educators who have similar values and interests allows for the development and exchange of ideas in a socially distributed manner. Educators engage in dialogue and reflection, collectively contributing to the development and refinement of instructional practices.
- ◆ *Sensitivity to values*: The emphasis on becoming sensitive to values and continually assessing growth and understanding along a continuum reflects the evolving biography of ideas. Educators' understanding of values and their manifestation in student learning evolves over time through reflection and experience.
- ◆ *Documentation and observation*: The use of tools such as the "Looking at Students' Thinking" protocol and the "Looking for Learning in the Wild" template encourages educators to document and observe instances of desired values in various learning environments. This process creates profiles of participation by capturing artifacts, interactions, and observations that demonstrate how values are expressed and fostered in practice.
- ◆ *Diverse educator cohort*: The case study highlights the inclusion of diverse educators from different educational contexts, including traditional classroom teachers,

independent schools, public schools, and out-of-school time educators. This commitment to diversity and inclusion promotes access and equity by ensuring that different perspectives and experiences are represented and valued in the cohort.

◆ *Mini-grants*: The provision of mini-grants to educators for the design process without constraints helps address potential resource disparities. This support enables educators to incorporate their values into their teaching practices and design learning experiences that align with their values, regardless of financial limitations.

Overall, Jeff and Peter's approach encompasses socially distributed idea development, the biography of an idea, profiles of participation, and considerations of access and equity. These elements are essential for fostering a participatory and inclusive learning environment.

Empowering Representation: Girls of the Crescent

This picture of practice explores the inspiring story of Girls of the Crescent—a project undertaken by Zena and Mena Nasiri, two Muslim girls who embarked on a mission to address the lack of representation and diversity in books available to them and their community. Their journey led them to establish the nonprofit organization Girls of the Crescent, dedicated to collecting and donating books with female Muslim main characters to schools and libraries. Through their participatory endeavors, Zena and Mena aimed to empower young Muslim girls and challenge stereotypes by providing them with relatable and inclusive literature.

Meet Zena and Mena

When Zena and Mena Nasiri walked into their local library in suburban Michigan as curious fourth-grade students, the sisters couldn't have imagined that moment would spark a remarkable journey, driven by a shared passion for reading and a desire for inclusivity. What began as a seemingly ordinary school

assignment evolved into an extraordinary story of empowerment and social change.

It all started when Zena and Mena were assigned a research
project on important historical figures. Eager to learn about the
Muslim women who inspired them, they discovered a scarcity of
books featuring such characters in their local public library. This
experience left a lasting impression on them, highlighting the
lack of representation and diversity in their reading materials.
It stayed with them as they progressed through their education
and, with the encouragement of their parents, educators, librarians, and local community, developed a deep passion for reading.

When asked about the influential figures who impacted their
story, Zena (20) and Mena (19) shared the importance of family and the support they received from both their mother and
father, who immigrated to the United States from Iraq in the
early 1990s. In an interview with Rochester Hills Mayor Bryan K.
Barnett, Zena explained, "Mom is really passionate about social
justice and advocating for people, and that's kind of where we
got that passion from, and our dad has always supported us."
Mena added, "And they're both big on education, and both big
on reading, so that's what kind of made us get into books too."[28]

When asked about their identities, both unsurprisingly
shared the importance of being Muslim females. After all, it was
this specific aspect of their identity that served as a catalyst for
the start of this project. Additionally, Zena explained:

> I'm also a part of the LGBTQ+ community and that's really
> important for me as a lot of people don't think that Muslim
> women and LGBTQ+ can exist simultaneously. But we defi-
> nitely do exist and that's a huge aspect of who I am.

For her part, Mena explained how her family's heritage influenced her perspective: "Being Middle Eastern, being from Iraq,
is a big part of my identity. You know, people sometimes group
Middle Easterners and Muslims together, but for me they're kind
of separate." The girls also agreed about the importance of considering different viewpoints and seeking to explore and appreciate diverse people and perspectives.

FIGURE 4.15 Girls of the Crescent co-founders, Zena and Mena Nasiri.
Illustration by Julie Rains.

Zena and Mena's Story

Zena and Mena's experience with participatory creativity surfaced organically as they, along with their mother Deyar Nasiri, began to explore the best way to create more inclusive representation in their Rochester community. After reading the book *The Lines We Cross* by Randa Abdel-Fattah,[29] which featured a relatable Muslim protagonist, Zena and Mena decided to take action. They began by advocating to have the book as an option in their local "Battle of the Books" competition and later decided to seek a more global impact. Zena explained the importance of that pivotal high school experience:

> Just being able to read a book with a character whose name was similar to ours. Her name is Mina. So it was the first time that Mena saw her name in a book and who had similar experiences and just whose daily life kind of resembles ours in the sense that she went to a mosque. She spoke her native language. She ate Middle Eastern food, and she experienced Islamophobia in the same sense that we did. And that kind of

brought us back to this experience in fourth grade where we couldn't find any books with female Muslim main characters. We decided that we had to do something to make these books more available so that little kids, little young Muslim girls, would be able to experience what we weren't able to experience.

Deciding to take action was the first step, but determining where to begin was the next challenge. That's when Deyar, the girl's mother, surfaced an interesting notion. "Why don't you do what Marley Dias did?"

In November of 2015, Marley Dias, now a student at Harvard University and renowned social justice advocate, launched the #1000BlackGirlBooks drive, utilizing the influence of social media to spread the word.[30] The goal of her campaign? To collect 1,000 books featuring Black female protagonists by February of the following year. The result? Astounding success. Not only did Dias accomplish her goal, but, according to her website, she has since collected over 13,000 books to date and has been featured in multiple high-profile news publications. Dias is supported by a rich network of "bloggers, schools, youth-focused organizations and millions of individuals who wanted to participate in the project."

In March of 2018, about three years later, Zena and Mena Nasiri, inspired by Dias, their mother, and their personal experiences, decided to launch a similar campaign, establishing the nonprofit organization Girls of the Crescent.[31] Initially, Zena and Mena did not envision establishing a nonprofit organization. Their primary goal was to make books with female Muslim main characters more accessible in their school libraries. Starting with a presentation to their school parent–teacher association (PTA), they secured initial funding and successfully collected over 200 books. The girls explained it was the overwhelmingly positive feedback and support they received from the PTA and the community that led them to officially register their organization as a nonprofit.

It changed my perspective of the community. I was expecting there to be more pushback and negativity around our cause, but there really wasn't any. Everybody was super support-ive, really positive, and everyone just kind of really wanted to help.

Though initially intimidated by the legal aspects and paperwork involved, they received guidance from their mother's friend, who had experience working with nonprofits. Determining their identity and name as an organization was another tricky element. "The name took us a really long time to think of," Zena explained, "We eventually landed on Girls of the Crescent because the cres-cent is a symbol of Islam, and then we're girls trying to help other girls so we thought it was really fitting." Local librarians, teach-ers, and the young feminist council also played a crucial role in their journey, providing advice, ideas, and support. Encouraged by this early success, Zena and Mena continued their efforts, expanding their reach through fundraising initiatives. To date, they have donated over a thousand books, locally, regionally, and even internationally. The girls have also been featured in prominent media outlets, including NPR Michigan Radio, *The Today Show*, *Elle* magazine, and Al Jazeera to name a few.

Representation in Process

Girls of the Crescent primarily raises funds to purchase books, ensuring a diverse range of titles that feature female Muslim main characters to support learners of all ages. In fact, the Nasiri family has even dedicated a room in their house as a designated "book room" to house the books in process. A question the girls regularly receive is how they are able to supply such a diverse range of books on such a specific topic. Zena explained:

> Female Muslim seems like a really specific and narrow topic and people think that there are only like two or three books out there. But in reality, there are so many female Muslims like in America, and there are so many female Muslims around the world, and a lot of them are writing these books because they themselves experience the same lack of representation. And the fact that these books aren't in the libraries, in schools, isn't because people are purposely avoiding them. I think it's just

because there's that lack of awareness, which is something that we're trying to raise awareness about as well.

While they purchase most books, they also receive donations from authors who resonate with their cause. To curate their collection, Zena and Mena conducted extensive research, creating a list of books categorized by age group. This list continues to grow, now comprising over 300 titles. Surrounded by stacks of colorful books of all shapes and sizes, Mena shared some of their favorite titles and series:

> This series is called the Yasmin Series by Saadia Faruqi and illustrated by Hatem Aly.[32] Every book is about this young Pakistani girl named Yasmin and she goes on a different adventure. In *Yasmin the Fashionista*, she tries on all of her mom's Pakistani clothing. It's a really fun book. The colors are great and in the back, there are facts about Pakistan and there are even some Urdu words you can learn.

In addition to the Yasmin Series, the girls highlighted *Golden Domes and Silver Lanterns* by Hena Khan and Mehrdokht Amini, *Amal Unbound* by Aisha Saeed, and *The Breadwinner* adapted by Cartoon Saloon, Melusine Aircraft Pictures, and Nora Twomey and written by Deborah Ellis.[33] Zena and Mena noted that community members and educators also contribute to the list, recommending books that align with Girls of the Crescent's mission.

The Impact

The impact of Girls of the Crescent extends beyond book donations. Zena and Mena have witnessed firsthand the excitement and appreciation of students when they visit schools and libraries to deliver books. Mena shared how that experience personally impacted the girls:

> Sometimes when we donate the books, we actually go into the schools and libraries and we get to see the students and sometimes, take photos and talk to them. And for both of us, that's really cool to actually see how excited they are looking

at these books and just seeing the actual impact that we're making.

Zena explained that librarians and teachers have shared stories of how these books have filled gaps in representation, enabling them to provide students with diverse perspectives:

> We've had a few librarians and teachers tell us that their students were asking for books like maybe with a Pakistani female character or with a character that they weren't able to provide because they couldn't find books with that kind of representation. And then when we were able to donate the books, and provide them our list, they realized that there were a lot more books available, and they were able to provide that representation for their students, which we think is really great.

By challenging stereotypes and combating stigmatization, Girls of the Crescent aims to foster a sense of belonging among young female Muslims and promote empathy and understanding among readers from various backgrounds. Zena and Mena are preparing to pass the torch to a younger generation of female Muslims, ensuring the sustainability of Girls of the Crescent. Zena, who is also heavily involved in advocacy work, explains:

> Something that I talk about a lot with different groups of people is student involvement and student advocacy. A lot of issues that districts are working on and teachers are focusing on directly impact students. And so, students should be the ones who are directly being involved in it. And if a young person sees a problem, and they have an idea of something to do about it, like how we saw a lack of diversity in books and we wanted to create a nonprofit, I think that their surrounding community of adults and teachers and schools should support them in every way to make that possible. Because a lot of the times, young people can feel like they don't really have the power to do things, and they might not really know

the logistics of it, but their ideas are still really important and their projects should be able to be successful.

As living proof of that sentiment, Zena and Mena are mentoring two young girls whom they hope will continue the organization's work in their own community. The girls both recognize the challenges they may face while balancing the demands of their college education at the University of Michigan but remain committed to supporting the cause.

Implications for Practice

Participatory creativity, as demonstrated by Zena and Mena, involves actively engaging individuals in the creative process to address social challenges. The Girls of the Crescent story reflects several key concepts associated with participatory creativity. First, Zena and Mena recognized the power of representation and diversity in literature, understanding that by providing relatable and inclusive stories, they could challenge stereotypes and empower young Muslim girls. This recognition led them to actively seek out and select books that highlighted the experiences of female Muslim characters.

Second, Zena and Mena embraced the concept of co-creation, illuminating the importance of socially distributed idea development. They engaged with their community, seeking input and recommendations for books that aligned with their mission. This included their local communities, such as their parents, teachers, and the PTA board, but also a broader community of contributors that they connected with through donations, book recommendations, and other means of organizational support. This may especially be the case in regard to involving others in the book selection process—which ensured a more comprehensive representation of diverse perspectives. Zena and Mena learned from the participatory process, just as their process was enhanced by others. As their idea sprouted from a small PTA grant into a nonprofit organization, their willingness to seek advice and input extended their impact to help more people on a broader scale.

Furthermore, Zena and Mena actively involved their peers, educators, and community members in their initiative, rallying support and creating a network of individuals invested in their cause. Through their book donations and visits to schools and libraries, they engaged with young readers, inspiring a love for literature and promoting empathy and understanding.

Finally, this picture of practice illustrates how both primary and secondary stakeholders can play various roles and have a lasting impact on the development of an idea. Beyond just Zena and Mena, a host of characters who contributed to the work in different ways may be developed by sketching the biography of the Girls of the Crescent idea. A quick sketch might look like this:

- ◆ Zena and Mena's story began with a school project, demonstrating the influence of their fourth-grade teachers in assigning the project and their local library in its limited book selection at that period in time.
- ◆ School would later have an influence again as the then high school students advocated to have *The Lines We Cross* by Randa Abdel-Fattah included in a "Battle of the Books" reading list.
- ◆ The sisters engaged their parents, seeking both support and inspiration from their own experiences as Iraqi immigrants, book enthusiasts, and educational supporters.
- ◆ In a brainstorming session, the family team was inspired by an outside actor, Marley Dias, a young advocate who lived in New York but whose story reached them via social media.
- ◆ From there, Zena and Mena actively sought support from their school PTA community, school educators, and librarians to curate their collection and ensure that it met the needs of their target audience.
- ◆ Their mother's friend helped them to structure and plan their nonprofit.
- ◆ Zena and Mena also embraced their peers by involving their classmates in their school's young feminist group and "Battle of the Books" organization.
- ◆ Local, national, and international press amplified their message, inviting participation from a wide range of people across the globe, including authors and illustrators who donated books in support.

◆ As Zena and Mena prepare to pursue their college education, they have already begun paving the way for future generations of young Muslim girls to continue the work of Girls of the Crescent. By mentoring younger girls, they are not only ensuring the sustainability of their organization but also fostering a spirit of leadership and activism among their peers—and setting up the next chapter of the biography of this idea to be written by a new host of authors.

The Girls of the Crescent picture of practice speaks loudly of the power of participatory creativity to address social issues and empower under-represented communities. Through their passion for reading and their commitment to challenging an obvious gap in literature, Zena and Mena took a lead role in harnessing the power of multiple stakeholders to create meaningful change. By establishing Girls of the Crescent, Zena and Mena not only collected and donated books but also fostered a sense of community, connection, and empowerment among young Muslim girls.

What's Your Story?

Writing this book has been an exciting experience for us, but writing this chapter has been especially riveting. We've enjoyed engaging with the practitioners and students mentioned above, hearing their stories, learning from them, and sharing with others. Perhaps some of the pictures of practice shared above directly relate to your own teaching and learning context, and you are compelled to try something out that you've just learned, experiment with a tool or practice that was shared, or tweak something from these narratives to suit your learning environment. Maybe these stories were not quite a good fit for where you work—but perhaps there have been some valuable takeaways within them that you can see being applied within your learning space.

However you related to these pictures of practice, we hope you've taken some inspiration away from this chapter—and we hope that inspiration is driving you to craft your own story. We would love to hear it!

As you consider bringing the work of participatory creativity into your classroom, we encourage you to read on to Chapter 5, where we offer a suite of tools that you can use in your practice.

Notes

1 Some of the quotes in this picture of practice come from Joyce's 2023 presentation for the 21st Century Learning Conference. To experience Joyce's presentation for yourself, see Pereira, J. L. (2023, May 9). Tracing stories of innovation: A human-centered approach to computer science (conference presentation). *21st Century Learning Conference*. Retrieved from https://www.21clconf.org/presentations/tracing-stories-of-ideas-a-human-centered-approach-to-computer-science/

2 For more about the Korea International School, see the About page of their website: https://www.kis.or.kr/about

3 For more on the art of coaching, see Aguilar, E. (2013). *The art of coaching: Effective strategies for school transformation*. Newark, NJ: John Wiley & Sons.

4 For more about Hawken School and their Creative Process Intensive course, see their website: https://masteryschool.hawken.edu/our-program/intensives

5 To view the Biodegradable case study referenced here, see (pp. 111–126) in the original *Participatory Creativity* book.

6 To learn more about the SEED framework, check out the SEED Framework website https://seedframework.com/ or read Jodie's encyclopedia entry on the SEED Framework in the *Springer Encyclopedia for Educational Innovation*: Ricci, J. L. (2020). The SEED framework for cultivating creativity (encyclopedia entry). In M. A. Peters & R. Heraud (Eds.), *Encyclopedia of educational innovation*. Springer Nature Singapore Pte Ltd. Retrieved from https://doi.org/10.1007/978-981-13-2262-4_106-1

7 See Ritchhart, R., & Church, M. (2020). *The power of making thinking visible: Practices to engage and empower all learners*. San Francisco, CA: Jossey Bass.

8 For more on the Mount Olympus perspective of creativity, see Gruber, H. E., & Davis, S. N. (1988). Inching our way up Mount Olympus: The evolving systems approach to creative thinking. In R. J. Sternberg (Ed.), *The nature of creativity: Contemporary psychological perspectives* (pp. 243–270). Cambridge, UK: Cambridge University Press.

9 To see the video about El Anatsui's bottle top work, visit https://www.youtube.com/watch?v=_d3RlE195Jl. And to learn more about El Anatsui and his work with bottle tops, see Goldberg, A. & Zunon, E. (2022). *Bottle tops: The art of El Anatsui.* New York: Lee & Low Books.

10 To learn more about Abstract: The Art of Design you can view the Netflix trailer: https://www.youtube.com/watch?v=DYaq2sWTWAA

11 To learn more about the practice of slow looking, see Tishman, S. (2017). *Slow looking: The art and practice of learning through observation.* New York: Routledge.

12 For more about the difference between these *I* and *we* paradigms of creativity, see Glăveanu, V. (2010). Paradigms in the study of creativity: Introducing the perspective of cultural psychology. *New Ideas in Psychology, 28*(1), 79–93.

13 See, for example, Berardo, K., & Deardorff, D. K. (2012). *Building cultural competence: Innovative intercultural training activities and models.* Virginia: Stylus Publishing, LLC; and Deardorff, D. (2006). Identification and assessment of intercultural competence as a student outcome of internationalization. *Journal of Studies in International Education, 13*(1), 241–266.

14 For more about the concept of competency-based learning, see Great Schools Partnership (2014, May 14). Competency-Based Learning. *The Glossary of Education Reform*, among other resources.

15 Note that all student names are pseudonyms.

16 To learn more about Bialik College, see About Bialik College on the school's website: https://www.bialik.vic.edu.au/about-bialik

17 To view an issue of *The Stories of Us*, visit https://sites.google.com/rcs-k12.us/origins/issues?pli=1

18 See Gladwell, M. (2000). *The tipping point: How little things can make a big difference.* Boston, MA: Little, Brown and Company.

19 See https://pz.harvard.edu/projects/cultures-of-thinking

20 For more about the work of John Hattie, see Hattie, J. (2023). *Visible learning: The sequel.* New York: Routledge.

21 To learn more about the Agency *by* Design framework for maker-centered learning, see Clapp, E. P., Ross, J., Ryan, J. O., & Tishman, S. (2016). *Maker-centered learning: Empowering young people to shape their worlds*. San Francisco, CA: Jossey-Bass or check out the Agency *by* Design website: http://www.agencybydesign.org/

22 A great resource for understanding the triadic theory of dispositions can be found in this seminal text: Perkins, D. N., Jay, E., & Tishman, S. (1993). Beyond abilities: A dispositional theory of thinking. *Merrill-Palmer Quarterly, 39*(1), 1–21.

23 To learn more about Ron Ritchhart's work on "Cultures of Thinking," see Ritchhart, R. (2015). *Cultures of thinking: The 8 forces we must master to transform our schools*. San Francisco, CA: Jossey Bass. To learn more about Stephen Covey's big rock analogy, see Covey, S. R., Merrill, A. R., & Merrill, R. R. (1996). *First things first*. New York: Free Press.

24 To learn more about the original "Looking at Students' Thinking" protocol, see Project Zero/Cultures of Thinking. (n.d.). *Looking at Students' Thinking (LAST) Protocol*. Retrieved from https://pz.harvard.edu/sites/default/files/LAST%2Bprotocol_New.pdf

25 To learn more about the "Looking for Learning in the Wild" tool, visit the Educator Resources section of the Agency *by* Design Pittsburgh website: https://www.agencybydesignpgh.com/

26 For more about Luma, see https://www.luma-institute.com/

27 To learn more about the "I Used to Think… Now I Think…" thinking routine, visit https://pz.harvard.edu/sites/default/files/I%20Used%20to%20Think%20-%20Now%20I%20Think_2.pdf

28 To listen to this conversation with Zena and Mena, visit https://www.buzzsprout.com/1725209/10673288

29 See Abdel-Fattah, R. (2016). *The lines we crossed*. New York: Scholastic Press.

30 To learn more about Marley Dias, visit her website: https://www.marleydias.com/

31 To learn more about the Girls of the Crescent organization, see https://www.girlsofthecrescent.org/

32 See https://saadiafaruqi.com/book-series/yasmin-series/

33 See Khan, H. (2012). *Golden domes and silver lanterns. A Muslim book of colors*. San Francisco, CA: Chronicle Books; Saeed, A. (2018). *Amal unbound: A novel*. New York: Nancy Paulsen Books; and Ellis, D. (2000). *The breadwinner*. New York: Oxford University Press.

5

The Participatory Creativity Tool Kit

OK, here we are at one of the most exciting parts of any educators' guide to anything: the tool kit! In order to cultivate a participatory creativity classroom, educators need a robust suite of tools, strategies, and resources at their disposal. In this chapter, we provide just that.

In the pages ahead, you will find that we have grouped 11 actionable tools under the headings of the four different key concepts associated with participatory creativity, as presented in Chapter 2: socially distributed idea development, biography of an idea, importance of role, and profiles of participation.

Each tool presented in each section follows a loose format—though some tools deviate in their structure from others. Generally speaking, you should expect to see a short description of each tool followed by a step-by-step suggested approach to that tool's use. After that, you'll find a load of information regarding when to use each tool, what each tool helps learners do, and tips for using each tool. Most tools also include an example or two on how the tool has been used by others—and every tool concludes with a *biography of the idea*, which provides a short history of the who and the how the tool was developed. Here, you may notice some familiar names—including many of the folks who appeared in the pictures of practice described in Chapter 4. You may see some new actors as well—educators who hail from

DOI: 10.4324/9781003136958-5

the broad participatory creativity community of practice who have helped design and shape these tools and strategies.

On a last note, while the following tools are designed in a stepwise format and include tips for implementing them, we want to give you permission to hack these tools to suit your specific context.

Enjoy the tools and have fun hacking!

Socially Distributed Idea Development

One of the fundamental aspects of participatory creativity is the socially distributed development of ideas. This key concept sheds light on the fact that creativity never takes place in isolation. Creativity is always socially and culturally situated. In other words,

FIGURE 5.1 Socially distributed idea development: creativity is always socially and culturally situated.

Illustration by Julie Rains.

the contributions of multiple stakeholders are crucial for innovation to flourish. This section of the tool kit aims to provide educators with strategies and resources to foster an environment where ideas are cocreated and developed in conjunction with multiple stakeholders, such as students, teachers, experts, and community members—or even technologies or other nonhuman actors. Throughout the tools that follow, we also recognize that conflict and tensions may arise in the creative classroom and that social mediation may be a necessary part of the participatory creativity process.

Stakeholder Mapping

A tool for shedding light on the various stakeholders who contribute to the development of creative ideas

Heralding larger-than-life individuals sends the message to young people that participating in creativity is just for the gifted few, making creative achievement seem out of reach for many young people. This tool encourages learners to think beyond the oversimplified narrative of the lone creative genius and instead consider the many stakeholders who contribute to the development of creative ideas.

When to Use This Tool?

This tool may be used to research historical innovations, especially those typically credited to a sole eminent figure. This tool may also be used to reflect on the collective participation of a group endeavor.

How to Use This Tool

1. **Choose** an idea for deeper analysis and place a written or visual description of the idea in a centrally located position (e.g., cubism, the light bulb, democracy, and hip-hop, etc.).
2. **Brainstorm** a list of the various stakeholders who may have contributed to this creative idea in response to the questions below. Consider including one suggested

stakeholder per sticky note (or other moveable recording tool):

    a. Who might have been the producers, those who led the charge?

    b. Who might have been the supporters, those who played behind-the-scenes roles?

    c. Who might have been the influencers, those who provided inspiration?

    d. Who might have been the intended audience, those for whom the idea was designed?

    e. What nonhuman actors or technologies might have also played a role in contributing to the development of this idea?

3. **Map out** the primary and secondary stakeholders. Place those who have had the closest active association with the development of the idea (the primary stakeholders) closest to the center, gradually tapering out to those who have had less direct association with the development of the idea (the secondary stakeholders) on the outer edges.

4. **Analyze** the map and consider these questions:

    a. What patterns or themes seem to be emerging and what might they reveal?

    b. What roles have the various stakeholders on your map played in the development of the idea?

    c. What representations are present in the stakeholders on your map? Are there over-representations or under-representations of any one social or cultural group that you notice? Why might this be?

5. **Reflect** on the learning process and consider these questions:

    a. How has this mapping of stakeholders shifted your understanding of the development of creative ideas?

    b. How might you see yourselves or the people you identify with in this map (or not)?

    c. How might you play a role in the development of creative ideas today and tomorrow? What roles might you play?

What Does This Tool Help Learners Do?

This tool encourages learners to look closely, explore complexity, consider different viewpoints, and reason with evidence to think beyond oversimplified narratives of creativity. An intentional effort to represent diverse cultural and social orientations toward creativity, coupled with a reduced emphasis on the achievement of the lone individual, can demonstrate that there is a role for all learners in the creative classroom.

Tips for Using This Tool

- ◆ It might be helpful to color-code the different kinds of stakeholders who emerge to reveal patterns as they may arise throughout the analysis. This will be a fluid process as learners build explanations and reason with evidence in speaking and/or writing to support their thinking.
- ◆ The process of jotting down stakeholders could be done individually, in silence with think time, in pairs or dyads, or as a whole group depending on the dynamics, needs, or preferences of learners.
- ◆ Contributing new stakeholders to the map should be encouraged as the analysis process goes forward and new connections are made.

Examples of This Tool in Action

Julie Rains has spent time exploring the concept of representation. She shared the biography of a light bulb, pointing out that while Thomas Edison was one iconic figure in the story of the light bulb's development, he was not the only stakeholder who contributed to the conception of the incandescent light bulb. Julie shared the story of inventor and draftsman Lewis Howard Lattimer, the person who patented the carbon filament which made the incandescent light bulb possible. From there, Julie connected to the picture book *Hidden Figures*,[1] sharing the story of a group of Black women who were also underrepresented throughout history. Her friend and colleague Kym Strozier also shared her experience and decision to leave the field of aerospace engineering because she didn't see any mentors who looked like her at the time. Using that discussion as a base, Julie read the story *Drawn Together*[2] and asked groups of four students to get together and write their own story. The catch? Three out of the four group members needed to remain silent throughout the whole process. The fourth and final member could talk, but their sole role was to travel to other groups, learn about what they were doing, and share it with their own group members as inspiration. At the conclusion of class, the group was asked to create their own stakeholder map of their book creation process, highlighting those individuals and ideas that inspired their creation. This process was meant to highlight the many individuals and influences that contribute to idea development.

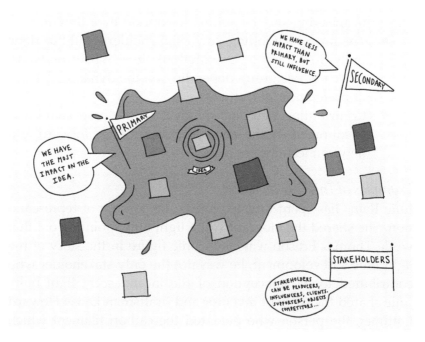

FIGURE 5.2 Stakeholder mapping. When engaging in the work of stakeholder mapping, it is helpful to consider the primary and secondary stakeholders who contribute to the development of creative ideas.

Illustration by Julie Rains.

Biography of This Idea

This tool was inspired by the collective efforts of Kym Strozier, Vidya Ganesh, and Julie Rains at Delta Kelly Elementary School in Rochester, Michigan. It was made even better through inspiration from Yerko Sepúlveda's exploration of artifacts in his Spanish classroom at Hawken School in Ohio. Finally, Sarah Sheya, founder of the JusticeXDesign Project, served as a thought partner throughout this tool creation process.

Successes, Challenges, Contributions, Actions

A tool for ensuring a generative group experience throughout the socially distributed idea development process

Engaging in the process of socially distributed idea development may be productive work but is not always easy. As with any social process, tensions may arise among individuals who arrive at the creative classroom with different personalities, working styles, or life histories. When social tensions arise, it is helpful to have a practice or protocol to deal with them. Or even better, before the class engages in the process of socially distributed idea development, put some ground rules in place to ensure that such tensions don't arise—or are easily addressed when they do.

When to Use This Tool?

This tool can be used as a proactive way of supporting positive group interactions or as a problem-solving tool to address challenges or tensions as they arise throughout the socially distributed idea development process.

How to Use This Tool

Notice and name that challenges or tensions are a natural part of the creative process and that pausing to reflect and address both our successes—as well as our challenges and tensions when they surface—ultimately makes us better and more productive as a community of learners.

1. If you are in the midst of a socially distributed idea development process, consider your group interactions, communications, process, and collective participation. What has been **successful**? How do you know?

   If you are about to commence a socially distributed idea development process, consider what has been successful for you throughout your experiences in similar processes in the past.

2. If you are in the midst of a socially distributed idea development process, what **challenges or tensions** might have surfaced for you and your peers along the way?

   If you are about to commence a socially distributed idea development process, consider what challenges or tensions have surfaced for you and your peers throughout your experiences in similar processes in the past.

3. If you are in the midst of a socially distributed idea development process, what have you and your peers done to make visible each team member's **contributions** to the work? What could the group better understand about you and your contributions? What could you seek to better understand about your group mates and their contributions?

   If you are about to commence a socially distributed idea development process, consider what you and your peers have done in the past to make visible each team member's **contributions** to the work? What have you and your peers done to best understand each person's contributions?

4. If you are in the midst of a socially distributed idea development process, what **actions** might the group need to take to improve its interactions, communications, processes, and/or collective participation? How will you know if the group makes progress in these areas?

   If you are about to commence a socially distributed idea development process, what systems might you put in place to maintain positive and productive group interactions—along with systems that may be in place to address social tensions if and when they arise?

What Does This Tool Help Learners Do?

Inviting multiple players to participate in idea development invites multiple personalities, making social navigation an important part of the creative process. Navigating social tensions is essential not only in the participatory creativity classroom but also throughout the creative economy. This tool provides learners the opportunity to pause and reflect on the arc of their experience (or past experiences), capturing the heart of the social interactions and considering steps to improve communications, processes, and participation.

Tips for Using This Tool

◆ Challenges are meant to surface general trends and are not meant to "call out" the behavior of specific individuals by name. Encourage learners to use more general language to keep the conversation focused on the collective participation of the group. In the words of our good friend Ron Berger: *Be kind, be specific, and be useful.*[3]

◆ To avoid "groupthink," encourage participants to take individual think time to document their own perspectives prior to sharing out with others. Support the consideration of multiple viewpoints and perspectives.

◆ This tool can also be used to support learners who might benefit from more scaffolded social interactions in the form of speech or social work interventions.

Examples of This Tool in Action

In Julie's media classroom in Rochester Hills, Michigan and in Erik Lindemann's third-grade classroom at Osborne Elementary School in Sewickley, Pennsylvania, students engaging in creative projects often ran into social tensions as they navigated the course of the work. The Successes, Challenges, Contributions, Actions tool was used as a means to document learners' processes and participation, reflecting on the things that went well and those that could be changed and adapted as the group continued its work over the course of time.

Biography of This Idea

This tool was inspired by the collective efforts of Kym Strozier, Vidya Ganesh, and Julie Rains at Delta Kelly Elementary School and Erika Lusky at Rochester High School in Rochester, Michigan. Additional contributions were made by Erik Lindermann and Matt Littell at the Quaker Valley School District in Pennsylvania.

The Stories of Us

A tool for making connections, seeking perspectives, and establishing a collective narrative

Throughout the creative process, learners may find many influential collaborators outside the walls of the creative classroom, encouraging the habits of perspective seeking and information sourcing to invite and understand a variety of viewpoints. This tool can be used to map multiple perspectives outside of the immediate classroom, valuing the expertise of a community of contributors.

When to Use This Tool?

This tool may be used to explore a topic that could be enriched by considering diverse viewpoints and perspectives across disciplines, generations, geographical regions, or genres.

How to Use This Tool

1. **Choose** an inquiry focus: a research topic, question, concept, or idea that your learners want to explore as a whole class, as individuals, or in small groups.
2. **Seek out perspectives.**
   a. Prompt your students to make a list of individuals they might contact to gain insight on their inquiry focus.
   b. Further prompt your students to select one or two people from their list and then contact them to seek their perspective on their inquiry focus. Have your students document their experiences with their first

contacts while asking those individuals to recommend at least one other person who might have an interesting perspective to share on the topic.

   c. Encourage your students to contact the folks who have been recommended, being sure to also document their experiences to bring back to the collective class.

3. **Organize and examine** the data and consider these lenses:
   a. Emergent categories and themes
   b. Contrasting points of view
   c. New questions that are coming to the surface

4. **Draw conclusions** and consider some of the following questions:
   a. What may have informed or impacted the perspectives of the people you spoke with?
   b. How might the perspectives of the people you spoke with inform or enrich your own perspective on the topic?
   c. How are all of these viewpoints connected? What story do they tell?
   d. What else does this information make you wonder? What new questions does it prompt?

5. Given what the learners have come to understand through the process described above, **what next steps** might they take to further their inquiry focus work.

What Does This Tool Help Learners Do?

This tool is designed to help students understand that there are many different sides to a story—that the various individuals who may have had common experiences may have different perspectives on those experiences. It further prompts students to understand that various actors contribute to the biography of an idea and that those actors may play different roles, come from different places, and hold different positions, but they are all connected. The learner may also see themself as a character in this narrative, playing their own role and holding their own perspectives.

Tips for Using This Tool

♦ Work with your students to ensure that their inquiry foci are nuanced and specific, that they are enhanced and informed by adding the perspectives of others, and that they are not simple questions that can be answered with a quick Internet search.

♦ This tool could be used to explore those excellent questions that are worth further investigation but that you don't have time to research during a class period.

♦ Contacts with people could take many forms, such as email, phone or video call, face-to-face meeting, and personal message on social media. It would be helpful for learners to consider those contacts who are likely to respond in a timely manner.

♦ The cycle of contact recommendations could repeat as many times as warranted within your curricular time frame and teaching and learning context.

♦ Written documentation of contact responses in the form of notes, interview transcripts, and so on is strongly encouraged to support the organization and examination of ideas.

Examples of This Tool in Action

In Rachel Mainero's middle school media center, learners were participating together in the creation of a student-generated magazine (see Socially Constructing the Origins of Us picture of practice in Chapter 4, pp. 122–127). Through the *Origins: The Story of Us* project, learners chose to research their family histories and then used those histories to publish creative works for their peers and community members. As part of that process, learners asked one family member to speak on a topic and then asked them to recommend another person who could speak on the same topic. This encouraged the students to dig deeper and provided a scaffold for qualitative research. Similarly, in Yerko Sepúlveda's high school Spanish classroom, Yerko encouraged learners to follow a similar process as they researched an area of their own interests both inside and outside of their classroom walls. He then suggested a method for learners to analyze the information they collected to generate a final project to share with the class.

Biography of This Idea

This tool was inspired by the collective efforts of Erika Lusky at Rochester High School, Rachel Mainero at Reuther Middle School, Yerko Sepúlveda at Hawken School in Ohio, and Julie Rains at Delta Kelly Elementary School in Rochester, Michigan.

What's Cooking?—and How Can I Help?

A tool for understanding and supporting quiet students in the creative classroom

Whether in the arts classroom, the math classroom, the English language arts classroom, or any other learning environment, many of us have had that experience of seeing students working in groups, wherein some students appear to be more active in their learning than others. At first glance, it may appear that some students are participating more than their peers. But a broader view of what it means to "participate" may lead us to understand that some students participate in learning in manners that are less visible—and perhaps less traditional—than others. The "What's Cooking—and How Can I Help?" tool was designed to better understand how the quiet students in our classrooms are engaging in their learning and then to consider how best to support them.

When to Use This Tool?

This tool can be used to support learners during a long-term group project, literature circle, science lab, creativity challenge, or any other classroom activity where learners are grouped together to achieve a common goal reliant on the participation of each member.

How to Use This Tool

While there is no one approach to supporting the quiet and less visibly active students in one's classroom, the "What's

Cooking—and How Can I Help?" tool offers a simple strategy: Just ask them how they are participating and what forms of participatory work are most engaging for them. To do this work, our colleague Miriam Ryan at Bialik College in Melbourne, Australia has posed an array of questions that have served as conversation starters for quieter students:

♦ When you are silently engaged with your peers, how are you participating? What thoughts are you contributing to the group, and how do you make those contributions?

♦ When you are excited and engaged in a learning experience, what are you doing? How might we bring aspects of those learning experiences into your work in this classroom?

♦ What do you see as your strengths as a learner? How can we build on those strengths in this classroom?

♦ What would make you most comfortable in this classroom? What do you need to fully participate in this space in a way that works best for you?

♦ How can we make your participation more visible to yourself and others?

Following a conversation based on these prompts, consider co-developing an individual participation plan for your quieter students. Be sure to check in and revisit that plan over time to see how well it is working—and what might need to be changed for it to be most effective.

What Does This Tool Help Learners Do?

The "What's Cooking—and How Can I Help?" tool serves as a means to gauge the thinking of students who may be more quiet and less visibly active in the classroom and then to co-develop entry points for engagement for those students. As the tool suggests, a student may not be contributing to a socially distributed creative learning experience in the ways one might expect, but that does not mean they are not participating. Rather, they are likely participating in ways that most suit their individual needs and interests.

Tips for Using This Tool

- ◆ Take time to observe students in groups and jot down what you notice prior to meeting with learners. This will give you some specific examples of what you are seeing to share with them as you create an individual participation plan.
- ◆ Consider student strengths and areas of growth and areas of passion. Be ready to share some suggestions in case the student isn't sure how they might want to contribute.
- ◆ Have an open mind as to what participation might look and sound like. Supporting students to contribute in unique ways is what participatory creativity is all about.
- ◆ Have high expectations for learners. Your belief of what they are capable of doing impacts their view of themselves as thinkers and learners.

Examples of This Tool in Action

In her arts classroom, Miriam Ryan has been experimenting with more participatory approaches to student learning. While she has found that students play various roles as they address the tasks that she presents to them, she has also puzzled over how to support students who appear to be participating less than their colleagues. Intuitively, Miriam understands that some students need to hang back, take it all in, and wait for their moment to participate. She recognizes that these students are indeed engaged in their learning and "doing the work," but their approach to participating in socially distributed learning environments may be less visible, more subtle, and more internal than that of their peers.

In Erika Lusky and Tarra Dodge's special education classroom, many of the students are nonverbal and use communication devices, such as iPads with core board vocabulary to share their thinking. To support their learning, Erika considers student strengths, interests, and how they might engage in more meaningful participation. By considering Miriam's questions through the lens of an educator prior to a lesson, Erika and Tarra are able to design learning opportunities that increase student voice and choice.

Biography of This Idea
This tool was inspired by Miriam Ryan and her arts classroom at Bialik College in Melbourne, Australia. It was enhanced through the efforts of Erika Lusky and Tarra Dodge in their self-contained cognitively impaired classroom at Rochester High School in Rochester, Michigan.

Biography of an Idea

Every idea has a story to tell. Reframing creativity as the biography of an idea is a concept within the participatory creativity framework that focuses on understanding and appreciating the journey an idea takes as it wends its way through the world. Along the way, many people—and even a host of nonhuman actors—contribute

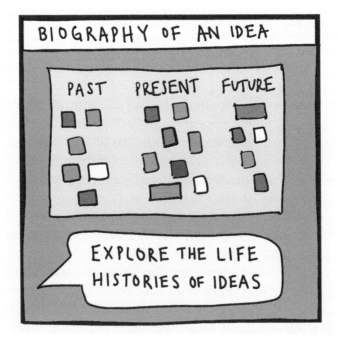

FIGURE 5.3 Reframing creativity as the biography of an idea makes visible the various actors who have contributed to the development of that idea—in unique ways—over time.

Illustration by Julie Rains.

to the development of an idea. Products are developed that serve as artifacts in the story of an idea, each advancing the narrative in some way. All of these plot points come together to tell a story, a biography, a life history of an idea as it takes shape over time. By exploring the biography of an idea, educators and students can gain valuable insights into the creative process and learn from past experiences to inform future endeavors.

From Individuals to Ideas

A tool for flipping the script on creativity by moving away from the narrative of creative individuals in favor of the life histories of the ideas those individuals are most known for.

Many of us are familiar with the traditional creativity narrative that lauds individuals for their groundbreaking contributions to a particular field of practice. But the truth is, no one individual may be responsible for any given creative idea. Creativity is always socially and culturally distributed. Wherever there is a creative icon held up for their genius, there is always a greater story to tell. The "From Individuals to Ideas" tool encourages students to think beyond the myth of the creative genius and instead consider a more systems-based perspective on distributed idea development.

When to Use This Tool?

This tool can be used as an introduction to systems thinking, as an extension to or in lieu of a traditional biography project, or as a means of exploring the complexities of historical figures. It can also be used as a means to provide an on-ramp to creative learning experiences for young people who don't identify as having the capacity to participate in creativity.

How to Use This Tool

1. Identify a popular creative icon (e.g., Isaac Newton, Toni Morrison, Steve Jobs, Ai Weiwei, etc.). Consider the products or ideas that person is most known for creating.

2. Select one product or idea that person is known for and then zoom out. Beyond the creative individual usually identified with this product or idea, what other actors or contributors might have participated in the development of this idea over time?

Consider some of the following questions:

♦ Who were the mentors, peers, and supporters of this creative icon at the time of their most significant contribution to this creative idea? Who were the mentors, peers, and supporters of this creative icon during the years before that?

♦ Who were the rivals or competitors of this creative icon at the time of their most significant contribution to this creative idea? Who were the rivals or competitors of this creative icon during the years before that?

♦ Who offered social or emotional support to this creative icon at the time of their most significant contribution to this creative idea? Who were the social or emotional supports of this creative icon during the years before that?

♦ What historical products preceded this idea? Who was responsible for creating those early products?

♦ Did something else need to be invented in order to make the development of this idea possible? If so, who or what was involved in the development of that other technology, system, or product?

♦ Is this idea still being developed today? If so, what new forms has it taken, and what new actors have been involved in its development?

♦ What social or cultural groups are prevalent in the development of this idea over time? What social or cultural groups seem to be missing from this story?

♦ Who are the hidden figures in the biography of this idea? What roles did those individuals play?

3. Develop a counternarrative that presents the biography of this idea rather than the story of one central figure. Be sure to include a variety of characters, groups of people,

or objects in your idea biography and note how each character, group of people, or object uniquely contributed to the development of this idea.

What Does This Tool Help Learners Do?

Heralding larger-than-life individuals sends the message that achieving greatness is just for the gifted few, making creative achievement seem out of reach for many young people. Orienting idea development as a system, rather than something attributed to one person, and zooming out to illuminate the rich landscape that informs idea development encourages learners to think beyond notions of genius or giftedness. Instead, reframing creativity as the biography of an idea makes visible the broader network of individuals who contributed to the development of those ideas over time—and the unique roles that they played. Furthermore, an intentional and concerted effort to represent diverse cultural actors and a social orientation toward creativity, coupled with a reduced emphasis on the achievement of the lone individual, can show that there is a role for all learners to play in the creative classroom.

Tips for Using This Tool

- ◆ You might begin by reading a traditional biography, highlighting areas that share information about the idea development rather than the main actor or finding books or other resources that focus on the development of ideas rather than a sole creative icon.
- ◆ Find other sources (e.g., interviews, articles, field trips, etc.) to consider different viewpoints, paying specific attention to those organizations that surface the contributions and stories of historically marginalized populations.
- ◆ The biography of an idea can take many forms. Some suggestions are comics, time lines, storyboards, skits or plays, or written narratives. Whatever you do, make it visible. Don't just talk about the biography of an idea with your students.

◆ Make it personal. As you and your students unearth the hidden figures within the biography of an idea, ask your students how they may connect with some of those hidden figures—and how they may likewise participate in the development of creative ideas in unexpected ways.

Examples of This Tool in Action

In Julie's media classroom, one student in each project took on the role of documenter, sketching the participation of the groups in a comic to capture snapshots of pivotal moments in the learning process. Students then applied this same idea as they explored traditional biographies and searched for other stakeholders who may have contributed to idea development over time. Creating a graphic representation spoke to their passion for graphic novels and introduced more participants (and their roles) to the creative process.

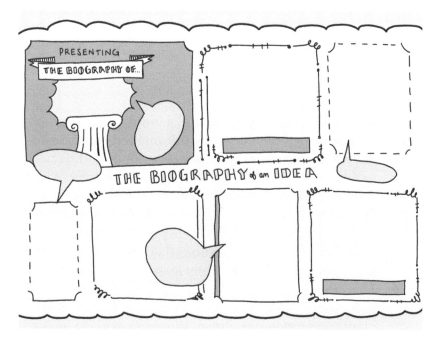

FIGURE 5.4 The "Individuals to Ideas" tool created by Julie Rains to support her students in seeing beyond lone creative individuals by mapping out the biography of an idea.

Illustration by Julie Rains.

Biography of This Idea

This tool was inspired by the collective efforts of Vidya Ganesh, Kym Strozier, and Julie Rains at Delta Kelly Elementary School in Rochester, Michigan. A special thank you to Jessica Ross and Erik Lindermann for their suggestions and feedback.

Looking Backward to Move Forward

A tool to help learners find future potential in past histories

The "Looking Backward to Move Forward" tool was designed to help learners find future potential in past histories. Creative ideas are manifested in the products that are developed to enact those ideas at any point in time during the ideas' history. This tool prompts learners to trace the biography of an idea through the succession of products that have been developed to enact that idea over time. The goal is for students to trace the succession of products associated with a particular idea all the way back to the original human need for that idea. Having gone through this process, learners are then prompted to leap back to the present and consider what the next iteration of that idea may be.

When to Use This Tool?

This tool may be used at the start of the creative product design process, before learners begin designing the next iteration of a particular product or service. It may also be used as a checking-in tool throughout the design process, to calibrate students to a particular human need, or story line for an idea.

Steps to Use This Tool

1. Identify a popular product or service associated with a particular market (e.g., the smartphone, a mobile ride-sharing service, etc.) that learners have an interest in further developing.
2. Once your students have identified a product or service of interest, prompt them to identify the broader idea that

this product or service may be associated with (e.g., tele-communication, mass transit, etc.).

3. Once they have done that, prompt your students to consider the human need at the heart of these broader ideas (e.g., to communicate over a distance, to get from place to place in a cost-effective and efficient manner, etc.)

4. Engage learners in the process of mapping out the past iterations of the products or services associated with the idea they have identified (e.g., flip phones, rotary phones, the telegraph, etc.; carpools, taxi cabs, street cars, horse carriages, etc.). Have students consider what might have been the benefits and shortcomings of each of the historical iterations they have identified.

5. As students trace the products or services associated with their focal ideas, encourage them to frequently revisit the human need (as they identified it earlier) that was meant to be addressed by each of these iterations.

6. Once your students have sufficiently traced the history of their idea far enough back in time, prompt them to work forward through their time line, always keeping the human need in mind.

7. When students arrive at the most recent iteration of the product or service they are interested in developing further (e.g., the most recent smartphone or mobile ridesharing service, etc.), have them compile the information they have gathered to consider how they may design a next iteration that builds on the knowledge they have gained through this process—and most importantly—addresses the human need at the heart of each of the past iterations of the products or services they have explored.

What Does This Tool Help Learners Do?

This tool helps learners consider how the different products associated with a particular creative idea have long histories rooted in human needs. By looking backward to the many iterations associated with a particular creative idea—and its original human need—learners are more apt to come up with a successful next iteration of that idea than if they had looked only at the most recent product associated with that idea.

Tips for Using This Tool

- ◆ Before engaging learners in the use of this tool, familiarize them with the "biography of an idea" concept to prime them for the research they will do.
- ◆ If possible, have young people work with or otherwise experience the past iterations of the product they intend to further develop (e.g., buy a past product at a yard sale or antique store, experience a past product at a museum, watch videos about past products online, etc.). They may put these products to work if they are still functional or take them apart to further explore their mechanics.
- ◆ Students may also interview family or community members who have used past iterations of the product (they intend to further develop) in order to get a sense of the benefits and shortcomings of these past products when they were in use. What might people miss about using these past products? How have the new products that replaced these past products changed their experiences? What aspects of the human needs associated with these products do these individuals feel are still unmet?
- ◆ Throughout the students' journey of tracing the biography of an idea through the past products associated with that idea, encourage learners to consider the different individuals associated with the development of those products along the way. To do this, you may consider using the "From Individuals to Ideas" tool (pp. 183–187).
- ◆ Make students' work visible. Have them use large chart paper and markers to map out the products or services they are exploring, develop time lines, and use other images to make their exploration visible.
- ◆ As students explore the biographies of the ideas they have identified, they may find themselves splintering their idea biographies into multiple sub-narratives leading to unexpected places. Rather than prompt students to stay on a single path, encourage them to explore multiple paths and then to follow the ones that are most interesting to them.

Biography of This Idea
This tool was first developed by Joyce Lourenco Pereira at the Atlanta International School in Atlanta, GA. Joyce originally used the tool to support innovation in her computer science classrooms and now uses them in her new role at Korea International School. To learn more, visit Finding Future Potential in Past Histories picture of practice in Chapter 4 of this book (pp. 72–80) to read about Joyce's classroom in action.

Surface a Wonder, Follow a Wonder

A tool for supporting curiosity through student-centered learning

Whether we teach first grade or high school physics, our curriculum can move at a fast pace—so fast that it may not leave enough room for student curiosity and wonder. The "Surface a Wonder, Follow a Wonder" tool emerged organically from a primary school teacher's classroom as a means to slow down the pace of a lesson and be more attentive to student interests and less concerned about sticking to the script. This pedagogical strategy prompts students to look for things that are interesting—things they wonder about—within their school content areas and then to go deeper with their wondering. Once wonders surface in the classroom, the "Surface a Wonder, Follow a Wonder" strategy prompts educators to follow their students' interests—and to let their students' curiosity lead the way.

When to Use This Tool?
This tool may be used at any point within a curricular arc, but likely more in the middle. It prompts students to develop the dispositions of wonder and curiosity and at the same time prompts educators to slow down and follow student interests when they surface.

How to Use This Tool

1. While exploring a topic in your curriculum, pause to ask students the following questions: *What do we know about this topic? What big questions do we have about this topic? What does this topic make us wonder about?*

2. After students have surfaced a sufficient number of won-ders about the topic they are studying, ask students, *Which of these wonders are we most curious about?* Allow students to vote or otherwise choose a wonder to further explore together as a class, or allow students to self-organize into smaller interest groups around the wonders they are most curious about.

3. Once students have determined the wonders they are most interested in, have them elaborate on their curiosity by asking, *Why are we interested in these particular wonders? What are we hoping to learn or understand by surfacing these wonders?*

4. Next, prompt your students to establish their own approach to inquiry by asking, *How might we follow these wonders further?*

What Does This Tool Help Learners Do?

This tool can be used to support curiosity and deeper learning in the classroom. Providing students with the opportunity to sur-face and explore the wonders they are most curious about—while establishing their own approach to inquiry—is a means of taking a student-centered approach to learning and fostering individual and collective agency. The "Surface a Wonder, Follow a Wonder" tool may be complemented by the "Think, Puzzle, Explore" think-ing routine from Project Zero's Visible Thinking project.[4]

Tips for Using This Tool

♦ As students brainstorm how they might follow their wonders, consider having them create specific, action-able goals.

♦ The pace of teaching and learning moves fast, and there is much content to cover. Try to carve out time for student wonder in your curriculum, so that students can go deep with the topics you are covering and have lasting learn-ing experiences.

♦ Develop a documentation strategy to make your stu-dents' wonders visible to themselves, their peers, and others.

♦ Frequently check in with your students about their wonders—the new discoveries they have experienced but
also how their wondering connects back to your central
curricular goals.

Examples of This Tool in Action
At Bialik College in Melbourne, Australia, primary school teacher
Naomi Ryan was exploring two big ideas with her students: *how
the past influences the present and how our actions today can change
the future.* During this unit, Naomi's students zeroed in on the
concept of climate change. Climate change was just one of several topics that Naomi had to explore within this unit, but rather
than quickly move through the topic, she chose to stay with it to
follow her students' curiosity. Climate change was a topic that
Naomi's students heard about all the time, but they had many
questions about the science associated with climate change—and
the role they might play in contributing to or preventing climate
change. To bring a greater awareness of this issue to her students,
Naomi used documentation to surface questions and puzzles her
students were struggling with, to make the concepts they won-
dered about visible.

Biography of This Idea
This tool was inspired by Naomi Ryan and her primary school
classroom at Bialik College.

Concept of Role

Roles play a vital part in a participatory creativity framework.
From this perspective, when individuals participate in creativity they do not do so in the same way but rather find different
pathways to engagement based on their skills, talents, background experiences, and cultural perspectives. The following
tools provide supports for educators to encourage their students
to play different roles in the process of socially distributed idea
development.

FIGURE 5.5 People play various roles when they participate in creative idea development. Illustration by Julie Rains.

Values, Needs, Trust

A tool for establishing trust during the creative idea development process

Creativity is not easy. It is hard and purposeful work. Participating in the creative process with others is even harder work—but it has great rewards. Before students engage in a creative pursuit, it is important to develop shared understanding and mutual respect so that each student may understand what other students in the process value and need—and what they have to offer. The "Values, Needs, Trust" tool suggests that students take turns sharing what they value and need, while understanding what their peers value and need, in order to develop the trust that is necessary to generatively engage in a process of distributed idea development.

When to Use This Tool?

This tool may be used as a norming strategy when introducing a topic, concept, project, or design challenge to proactively foster positive interactions among a group of students. It may also be used as a check-in tool at several times in the process, to gauge how a group is performing and to address any social tensions that may be in the air.

How to Use This Tool

Introduce a topic, concept, project, or design challenge.

Through the lens of the topic, concept, project, or design challenge, students individually take time to reflect on a series of "I" questions, jotting down their thinking for later reference.

I

◆ What am I interested in?
◆ What do I care about?
◆ In what ways do I need to feel supported, heard, and respected?

After quiet reflection time, students meet with their partners, groups, and/or class and use a series of "You" questions to seek information from their peers. All students have the chance to share their "I" thinking and then jot down the "You" thinking as they listen to their peers' responses.

YOU

◆ What are you interested in?
◆ What do you care about?
◆ In what ways do you need to feel supported, heard, and respected?

Once all students have shared, the group makes connections together and uses that information to consider how they might include the collective's interests, values, and needs to develop a deeper understanding of the class topic, concept, project, or design challenge. They do this by using the "we" voice to address the same prompts.

WE
- ◆ What are we interested in? How might we connect our interests to deepen our understanding?
- ◆ What do we care about? How will that be reflected in our creative process?
- ◆ In what ways do we need to feel supported, heard, and respected? How will we make that happen?

Beyond just surfacing interests, needs, and mechanisms for support and respect, a final step of this tool may be to articulate what roles participating students may play in order to live up to the answers to the "we" questions presented above.

What Does This Tool Help Learners Do?

This tool fosters a safe and supportive environment, encouraging learners to take time to experiment, make mistakes, and push their own thinking and learning. Educators in the creative classroom can encourage learners to enact their individual agency throughout the creative process in ways that capitalize on the best that each individual has to bring to the process. This tool encourages each student to be able to see themselves in the pursuit of the greater collective, recognizing their strengths, passions, and talents.

Tips for Using This Tool

- ◆ This tool can be used in pairs or small groups or as a whole class to develop shared trust. If you are planning to use this with a whole class, it would be helpful to create small groups to complete the "You" section of the tool together first, before sharing their thinking with the larger collective to develop a more in-depth conversation.
- ◆ After trust is generated, it is helpful to create the time and space to experiment and engage with both one's own areas of interest as well as the new ideas of others and experiment/self-correct throughout the creative process.
- ◆ Post the documentation of this tool and create periodic opportunities for learners to check in with one another

to make sure their needs are still being met and that their interests and values are being represented in the larger collective, perhaps through this tool or by means of the "Successes, Challenges, Contributions, Steps" tool presented earlier in this chapter (see pp. 173–176).

Examples of This Tool in Action

At the Project Zero Classroom at the Harvard Graduate School of Education, Dolph Hardigree and Erika Lusky used this tool to encourage the development of a positive learning community in their educator study group. The adult participants took turns answering each of the questions silently in writing first and then shared out to identify key themes from the group.

Biography of This Idea

This tool was inspired by the collective efforts of Erika Lusky at Rochester High School in Rochester, Michigan; Nate Hatt and Jeff Kupperman at A2 STEAM in Ann Arbor, Michigan; and Kym Strozier and Julie Rains at Delta Kelly Elementary School in Rochester.

Attitudes, Attributes, Actions

A tool for supporting engagement and student agency

Within any classroom, there are a variety of ways for students to participate in their learning. Nonetheless, sometimes students have trouble finding an entry point to engagement within a particular lesson or unit of study. The "Attitudes, Attributes, Actions" tool was developed by teachers at Bialik College in Melbourne, Australia to surface multiple entry points to engagement for students and to provide them with options for how best they might participate in the classroom.

When to Use This Tool?

This tool may be used at the beginning of a creative idea development project—or along the way to help students re-calibrate and adjust to a particular task at hand.

How to Use This Tool

1. Introduce your students to a particular concept that they will be studying, a project they will be developing, or a design challenge for them to take on.
2. Working in small groups, ask your students what **roles** they may need to play to address this concept, project, or challenge (e.g., an experimenter, a project manager, a communicator, etc.).
3. Having identified a set of roles, ask your students what **attitudes** they will need to take on in order to play each of these roles (e.g., we'll need to be curious, we'll need to think critically, we'll need to be active listeners, etc.).
4. Next, ask your students what might be the **attributes** associated with each of these attitudes (e.g., what does it mean to be a curious person? what does it mean to be a critical thinker? what does it mean to be an active listener?).
5. Finally, have your students consider what **actions** they may take to begin their project work, based on the attitudes and attributes they have discussed.

What Does This Tool Help Learners Do?

This tool has been designed to help students carefully consider the roles that they will need to play in order to engage with a particular concept, project, or design challenge. It encourages engagement and student agency by providing multiple pathways for participation and making them visible. By choosing a set of attitudes, attributes, and actions to pursue throughout a lesson or unit of study, students are encouraged to take more control over their learning experiences. One of the goals for this tool is to break down barriers to entry for students by providing them with pathways to learning that are based on the strengths and interests they bring with them each day.

Tips for Using This Tool

◆ As students work through the various steps of the tool, it may be helpful to have them use chart paper and markers to make their thinking visible. Students can also use sticky notes to sketch out their ideas, group them together, and make connections.

♦ Consider combining the use of this tool with the "Values, Needs, Trust" tool presented earlier in this chapter (see pp. 193–196).

Examples of This Tool in Action

At Bialik College, English and history teacher Justine Smith, Jewish studies teacher Sharonne Blum, and mathematics teacher Jennifer Kain each experimented with variations of "Attitudes, Attributes, Actions" in their separate classrooms. The three teachers informally discussed the tool on several occasions and then observed the tool in action in one another's classrooms. While Jennifer used the tool with its three prompts for her older students, Justine and Sharonne have pared the tool down to "Attitudes and Actions" when working with their younger students. In addition to the formative conversations these three teachers had about the tool, "Attitudes, Attributes, Actions" was also born of Justine's interests in dispositional thinking and explicit instruction and supported by concepts she gleaned from articles about effective teamwork.

Biography of This Idea

The "Attitudes, Attributes, Actions" tool is based on the work of Justine, Sharonne, and Jennifer at Bialik College and largely modeled off of the structure that Justine originally established for her classroom.

Profiles of Participation

When young people engage in creative idea development, they play different roles, but those roles are neither fixed nor unidimensional but rather multiple and dynamic. The various roles that young people play in the participatory creativity classroom comprise their profile of participation. The tools in this section help shed light on the contributions of individuals within a

FIGURE 5.6 Young people and adults play different roles when they participate in the development of creative ideas, but those roles are neither fixed nor unidimensional but rather multiple and dynamic.

Illustration by Julie Rains.

participatory creativity endeavor. These tools have been designed to support young people in developing a more comprehensive understanding of the roles they play in the creative classroom and the impact they have on the creative process.

Participation Tracker

A tool for making student participation visible

The "Participation Tracker" was developed to make student participation visible. Most specifically, it was designed to illustrate students' emergent profiles of participation. In this way, the "Participation Tracker" has the potential to support young people as learners and creative agents by highlighting their strengths and shedding light on their opportunities for growth.

When to Use This Tool?

The "Participation Tracker" can be used throughout any participatory learning experience and is best used when employed over time. The "Participation Tracker" can further be used to orient students to their strengths and to encourage them to take on new roles within any given socially distributed learning experience. It may further be used as a formative assessment tool to gauge student participation and prompt further development.

How to Use This Tool

In the most general sense, the "Participation Tracker" is a simple table that consists of a list of student names across an upper row and a list of roles along the far-left column (see Table 5.1). The tool can be used in a variety of ways—as a teacher observation tool, as a student self-assessment tool, or as a peer-assessment tool. The "Participation Tracker" can be used in the moment to document student participation or shortly after a learning experience as a reflection tool—or even as an exit ticket.

The above table presents the basic structure of the "Participation Tracker," but this structure can be tweaked or adapted in a variety of ways. While the names of the students are meant to be replaced by the names of the students within a classroom, or more likely within a small group in a classroom, the roles listed in the column on the far left may be variable.

TABLE 5.1 The Standard Template for a "Participation Tracker"

Roles	Student Participation Tracker						
	Student 1	Student 2	Student 3	Student 4	Student 5	Student 6	Student 7
Role 1							
Role 2							
Role 3							
Role 4							
Role 5							
Role 6							

Design by Edward P. Clapp

Both Erik Lindemann and Lee Howard have used the roles that were originally listed in the *Participatory Creativity* book. Other educators have used this tool with a blank column of roles to begin with and then filled in role descriptors as those roles emerged through students' work.

To use the tool, some educators have placed a tick mark to indicate when a student has played a certain role during a lesson or over the course of a unit. Other educators have placed tally marks for each time a student enacted a particular role during a lesson or over the course of a unit. The columns below a student's name can be interpreted as that individual's profile of participation—indicating the various roles they have played when they have engaged in a particular lesson or unit of study. The rows following each role indicate the array of individuals who have enacted a particular role.

However the "Participation Tracker" is used, it is ultimately meant to be employed as a conversation starter for a discussion with students about how they participate in their learning experiences and what their profile of participation looks like.

What Does This Tool Help Learners Do?

The "Participation Tracker" supports students in understanding the many ways that they participate in their learning experiences by making their participation in learning—especially as it pertains to creative idea development—visible. This tool can further be used to illustrate a student's emergent profile of participation. When used as an observation tool by either teachers or students, it fosters close looking and careful attention to the roles that various individuals play in a distributed learning experience. When used as a self-assessment tool, the "Participation Tracker" supports young people in reflecting on their own experiences and especially the way in which they participate in those experiences. Most powerfully, the "Participation Tracker" provides a window into who students are as participants in the classroom—or a mirror for seeing and understanding oneself as a multifaceted contributor to idea development within individual and group-based learning environments.

Tips for Using This Tool

♦ Familiarize your students with the concept of a profile of participation. This may be an unfamiliar concept for many students.

♦ To get the most out of the "Participation Tracker" tool, routinize its use within your teaching and learning environment. The more you and your students become familiar with the use of this tool, the more it will become second nature to record student participation on the tool as well as to interpret that information later on.

The Biography of This Idea

This tool was inspired by the tables developed by Edward and presented in the original *Participatory Creativity* book. It was further developed by the collective efforts of Matt Littell at Quaker Valley High School and Erik Lindemann at Osborne Elementary School in Sewickley, Pennsylvania with further contributions offered by Lee Howard at Bialik College in Melbourne.

Participation Mapping

A tool for documenting student participation during a socially distributed idea development experience

Developing the sensitivity to our own participation and the participation of others is a crucial aspect of navigating both the creative classroom and creative economy. This tool encourages students to pause and reflect on who is participating and how they are participating during any given idea development experience. It also makes thinking visible as documenters draw images and jot down quotes and thoughts based on student interactions.

When to Use This Tool?

This tool may be used at multiple times and in multiple settings, including during classroom discussions, literature circles, group projects, or creativity challenges. It can also be used with adult learners during staff meetings, professional learning experiences, or other collective endeavors.

How to Use This Tool

A group of students engage in some form of socially distributed project work over a period of time while a documenter (teacher or classmate) records their work. Typically, the group interacts naturally while the documenter silently observes, rather like an ethnographer or naturalist. After the work session is complete, the documenter shares their observations with the group—and the group reflects on their experiences.

◆ **Participate**: Students engage in a socially distributed learning activity. Ideally, they will speak, write, act, craft, or participate as they would without someone observing and documenting.

◆ **Document**: A documenter (e.g., teacher, classmate, colleague, etc.) describes what they notice, recording all ideas and paying specific attention to words, actions, body posture, and so on. The documenter should try to refrain from judgment, interpretations, or assumptions. There will be time later to infer, explain, and reflect.

◆ **Connect**: The documenter shares what they noticed and the group makes connections. The group then considers if other perspectives or ideas need to be added.

◆ **Reflect**: The group reviews what's been shared and considers how what they noticed impacted each student's process and participation. The students then jot down key ideas from the conversation for future action.

What Does This Tool Help Learners Do?

This tool helps learners increase their sensitivity to participation in the classroom. By helping learners proactively discuss multiple ways of being, participating, and navigating uncertainty, this tool supports young people in valuing the contributions of each student in the creative process.

Tips for Using This Tool

♦ Have all learners practice the art of documentation before asking them to document "on the fly." This will create space and time for a discussion of the difference between noticing and interpreting.

♦ Share a variety of examples of what documentation might look like (e.g., drawings, lists, videos, pictures, etc.), encouraging documenters to consider which methods support how they learn best.

♦ Prior to having the documenter share, be sure to set boundaries on how the sharing experience will go. Sharing may work best when the documenter offers an initial share-out while the other participants listen silently. Then the connect phase creates the opportunity for a whole-group discussion.

Examples of This Tool in Action

In Julie Rains and Erika Lusky's middle school resource classroom, students would engage in "Dinner Table Discussions" surrounding classroom texts. Erika and Julie would take turns as the documenter to jot down the thinking and interactions of their learners. Inspired by Edward's Creativity Challenge workshops, Julie and Erika began to use adaptations of this tool to document a group's participation in the creative process in both the classroom and professional learning settings.

Biography of This Idea

This tool was inspired by the classroom work of Julie Rains and Erika Lusky at West Middle School in Rochester, Michigan. It was later enhanced through the inspiration of Edward's Creativity Challenge workshops at several Project Zero Perspectives conferences, especially his session at the International School of Amsterdam.

FIGURE 5.7 The "Participation Tracker" tool for documenting student participation during a socially distributed idea development experience.

Using Pedagogical Tools in Your Context

Throughout this chapter, we've considered specific tools and general best practices to foster the development of participatory creativity in a teaching and learning environment. To effectively use the tools and practices mentioned in the Participatory Creativity Tool Kit in your own context, consider the following ten steps:

1. *Familiarize yourself*: Take the time to understand each tool, strategy, and practice presented in the tool kit. Familiarize yourself with the concepts of socially distributed idea development, the biography of an idea, the concept of role, and profiles of participation.
2. *Adapt to your context*: Every educational environment is unique, so tailor the tools and practices to suit the specific needs, goals, and constraints of your classroom or learning setting. Consider the age group, subject matter, and

the dynamics of your students when implementing new tools.

3. *Introduce gradually*: Start by introducing a few selected tools and strategies at a time. Gradually incorporate them into your teaching methods and observe how they resonate with your students.

4. *Provide guidance*: Offer clear instructions and guidance when introducing new tools or practices. Help students understand the purpose and expected outcomes of each activity.

5. *Encourage reflection*: Promote reflective discussions and self-assessment among students. Encourage them to think critically about their creative process and growth.

6. *Foster a safe environment*: Create a safe and inclusive learning environment where students feel comfortable sharing ideas, taking risks, and embracing setbacks and missteps as learning opportunities.

7. *Celebrate progress*: Recognize and celebrate the efforts and progress of students as they engage with the participatory creativity tools. Positive reinforcement can boost motivation and confidence.

8. *Participate with colleagues*: Collaborate with other educators or colleagues to share experiences and insights. Discuss how the tools are working in different contexts and learn from each other's experiences.

9. *Collect feedback*: Regularly gather feedback from students on the effectiveness of the tools and practices. Use this feedback to make improvements and adjustments to better suit the needs of your students.

10. *Stay open to innovation*: Embrace a growth mindset and be open to experimenting with new tools and practices. The field of participatory creativity is continually evolving. Staying open to innovation is crucial.

The Participatory Creativity Tool Kit is a resource to support and enhance your teaching practices, but ultimately your passion and dedication as an educator will make the most significant impact on fostering creativity and participation in your classroom.

Be patient and persistent, as cultivating a participatory creativity environment may take time, but the rewards in student engagement and innovative outcomes will be well worth the effort.

Notes

1 See Shetterly, M. L. (2016). *Hidden figures: The untold true story of four African-American women who helped launch our nation into space.* New York: Harper.
2 See Lê, M. (2018). *Drawn together.* New York: Disney-Hyperion.
3 For more about Ron Berger's work, see https://eleducation.org/about/staff/ron-berger
4 To learn more about the *Think, Puzzle, Explore* thinking routine, see https://pz.harvard.edu/sites/default/files/Think%20Puzzle%20Explore_1.pdf

6

Conclusion

In a dimly lit classroom, a group of students huddle around a table, their faces illuminated by the glow of their digital devices. They are engaged in a dynamic conversation, brainstorming ideas, and planning a project that combines art, technology, and social activism. Students are seeking to create an app that identifies community recycling centers, mapping the most convenient zones for each part of the city. Using Procreate on her iPad, one student is sketching graphics to accompany a digital map, while her groupmates are working on programming the app itself. The atmosphere is electric as these students tap into their collective imagination and harness the power of participatory creativity.

The Future Potential of the Creative Classroom

As we look ahead, the future potential of the creative classroom is nothing short of remarkable. Participatory creativity offers a pathway for students to become active agents of change, navigating a world that is increasingly complex and interconnected. The practices and principles discussed in this book lay the groundwork for a future where creativity is not confined to the realm of the arts but becomes a core driver of innovation across disciplines.

By establishing a participatory creativity classroom, educators are sowing the seeds for a generation of mulitmodal learners who will transcend boundaries and build systems upon systems

DOI: 10.4324/9781003136958-6

that connect cultures, perspectives, and economies. The skills and mindsets cultivated within this environment go beyond mere academic achievement; they empower students to engage with the world, tackle real-world challenges, and shape a future that is inclusive, sustainable, and just.

But a quick note on the word "potential"—a word we've been throwing around a bit here. Yes, we see great potential for the work of participatory creativity in the decades to come. In fact, we firmly believe that a participatory approach to invention and innovation will be the only future way forward within our increasingly connected and globally expanding worlds. In the here and now as well as in the not-so-distant future, a participatory approach to engaging in the world will be essential for success in life and work not only in terms of the social and cultural interactions we experience but also in terms of our engagements with new technologies—that are already becoming our participatory partners today.

That being said, the word potential has a bad rep among many in the field of creativity studies. It harkens back to the creativity tests of the 1960s, 1970s, and 1980s which sought to measure young people's creative potential based on narrow psychometric scales—and then track them toward creative fields while tracking other students elsewhere. The core principles of participatory creativity growl and bristle against such practices. Indeed, we are aware of the tension around the word potential. We are also aware that many have argued that the use of the word potential looks forward for opportunity without recognizing the opportunity that sits before us right now.[1] *There is so much potential in the here and now—why must we fret about the future?* We further understand this argument—and respect it deeply.

But all that being the case, here we intend to reclaim the word potential. We assert that there is great potential for the employment of a more participatory approach in education and across all professional sectors today and that we should harness that potential. At the same time, the potential we see for participatory creativity should not be limited to this current moment. Instead, it should be further cultivated for the future.

It's dangerous to try to predict the future. As any researcher will tell you, you should never try to predict beyond your data. But we're going to take a risk here and argue for the future potential of participatory creativity in the decades ahead—to support all of the jobs and technologies of the future that everyone says that we cannot even imagine today.

Next Frontiers for Participatory Creativity

As we venture into uncharted territories, the next frontiers for participatory creativity await our exploration. The convergence of emerging technologies, such as virtual reality, artificial intelligence, and augmented reality, offers great opportunities for transforming the creative classroom (see Figure 6.1). Imagine students

FIGURE 6.1 Virtual reality, artificial intelligence, and other emergent technologies offer great opportunities to support teaching and learning in the participatory creativity classroom.

Illustration by Julie Rains.

immersing themselves in virtual worlds, participating with peers from different cultures and backgrounds, and co-creating solutions to global issues.

Furthermore, participatory creativity has the power to transcend the confines of traditional educational settings. The digital age has opened up new avenues for learning, and online platforms and communities offer opportunities for students to engage in participatory creative practices on a global scale. The democratization of knowledge and tools allows students to connect, share, and learn from one another, transcending geographical boundaries and enriching their creative experiences.

As we conclude this book, we are reminded of the limitless possibilities that participatory creativity holds. It is not merely a pedagogical approach or a set of practices; it is a mindset that fosters curiosity, resilience, and empathy. It is a catalyst for innovation, social change, and personal growth.

The future of participatory creativity beckons us to embrace its potential, to reimagine education as a dynamic ecosystem where students are active participants in their learning journeys—and everyone has a role to play. Let us embark on these journeys together, forging new paths, and unlocking the creative potential within ourselves and the next generation. The time for participatory creativity is now.

Note

1 Our good friend, mentor, and colleague Michael Hanchett Hanson has spoken much on this topic—and we have learned a great deal from him.

References and Suggestions for Further Reading

Below we have collected a variety of references that have been cited throughout this book and that you may be interested in pursuing for further reading. Many of these books, articles, and other publications have been directly referenced in the chapters above, while others are listed here for those of you who may be interested in further reading. If you are one of those curious critters, as you engage with the materials below, we encourage you to *follow your wonder* by further pursuing the works cited at the end of these sources. You never know where one reference may lead you!

Abdel-Fattah, R. (2016). *The lines we crossed*. New York: Scholastic Press.

Aguilar, E. (2013). *The art of coaching: Effective strategies for school transformation*. Newark, NJ: John Wiley & Sons.

Amabile, T. M., Colins, M. A., Conti, R., Phillips, E., Picariello, M., Ruscio, J., & Whitney, D. (1996). *Creativity in context*. Boulder, CO: Westview Press/Perseus Books Group.

Bandura, A. (2000). Exercise of human agency through collective efficacy. *Current Directions in Psychological Science, 9*(3), 75–78.

Bandura, A. (2006). Towards a psychology of human agency. *Perspectives on Psychological Science, 1*(2), 164–180.

Berardo, K. and Deardorff, D. K. (2012). *Building cultural competence: Innovative intercultural training activities and models*. Virginia: Stylus Publishing, LLC.

Blythe, T., Allen, D., & Powell, B. S. (1999). *Looking together at student work*. New York: Teachers College Press.

Blythe, T., et al. (1999). *The teaching for understanding guide*. San Francisco, CA: Jossey-Bass.

Bourdieu, P., & Passeron, J. (1977). *Reproduction in education, society, and culture*. Beverly Hills, CA: Sage.

Clapp, E. P. (2016). *Participatory creativity: Introducing access and equity to the creative classroom*. New York: Routledge.

Clapp, E. P. (2019a). Five lessons learned about creativity. *Creative Teaching and Learning*, 8(4), 66–72.

Clapp, E. P. (2019b). Introducing new voices to the creativity studies conversation: W. E. B. Du Bois, double-consciousness, and *The Souls of Black Folk*. In V. P. Glăveanu (Ed.), *The creativity reader* (pp. 543–559). New York: Oxford University Press.

Clapp, E. P. (2020). Don't call it collaboration!: Reframing success in teams from the perspective of participatory creativity. In R. Reiter-Palmon, A. McKay, & J. C. Kaufman (Eds.), *Creative success in teams*. Series: Explorations in creativity research (J. C. Kaufman, series editor) (pp. 101–121). Cambridge, MA: Academic Press.

Clapp, E. P. (2022). Participation (encyclopedia entry). In V. P. Glăveanu (Ed.) *Palgrave encyclopedia of the possible* (pp. 966–974). Singapore: Springer Nature.

Clapp, E. P., & Hanchett Hanson, M. (2019). Participatory creativity: Supporting dynamic roles and perspectives in the classroom. In R. Beghetto & G. E. Corazzo (Eds.), *Dynamic perspectives on creativity: New directions for theory, research, and practice in education* (pp. 27–46). Cham, Switzerland: Springer.

Clapp, E. P., & Kamilah, A. (2019). Critical lenses for progressive education. In: M. Peters & R. Heraud (Eds.), *Encyclopedia of educational innovation*. Singapore: Springer. https://doi.org/10.1007/978-981-13-2262-4_109-1

Clapp, E. P., Ross, J., Ryan, J. O., & Tishman, S. (2016). *Maker-centered learning: Empowering young people to shape their worlds*. San Francisco, CA: Jossey-Bass.

Covey, S. R., Merrill, A. R., & Merrill, R. R. (1996). *First things first*. New York: Free Press.

Csikszentmihaly, M. (1988). Society, culture, and person: A systems view of creativity. In R. J. Sternberg (Ed.), *The nature of creativity* (pp. 325–339). New York: Cambridge University Press.

Csikszentmihalyi, M. (1999). Implications of a systems perspective for the study of creativity. In R. J. Sternberg (Ed.), *Handbook of creativity* (pp. 313–335). Cambridge, UK: Cambridge University Press.

de Novais, J. (2023). *Brave community: Teaching for a post-racist imagination*. New York: Teachers College Press.

Deardorff, D. (2006). Identification and assessment of intercultural competence as a student outcome of internationalization. *Journal of Studies in International Education*, 13(1), 241–266.

Delpit, L. (1988). The silenced dialogue: Power and pedagogy in educating other people's children. *Harvard Educational Review*, *58*(3), 280–298.

Delpit, L. (2006). *Other people's children: Cultural conflict in the classroom.* New York: The New Press.

Diderot, D. (1867). *Paradoxe sur le comédien.* Paris, France: Bibliothèque Nationale.

Ellis, D. (2000). *The breadwinner*. New York: Oxford University Press.

Gardner, H. (1983). *Frames of mind: The theory of multiple intelligences.* New York, NY: Basic Books.

Gardner, H. (1993a). A multiplicity of intelligences. *Scientific American Presents, Exploring Intelligence*, *9*(4), 19–23.

Gardner, H. (1993b). *Creating minds: An anatomy of creativity seen through the lives of Freud, Einstein, Picasso, Stravinsky, Eliot, Graham, and Gandhi.* New York, NY: Basic Books.

Gladwell, M. (2000). *The tipping point: How little things can make a big difference.* Boston, MA: Little, Brown and Company.

Glăveanu, V. (2010). Paradigms in the study of creativity: Introducing the perspective of cultural psychology. *New Ideas in Psychology*, *28*(1), 79–93.

Glăveanu, V. P. (2010). Creativity as cultural participation. *Journal for the Theory of Social Behaviour*, *41*, 48–67.

Glăveanu, V. P. (2014a). *Distributed creativity: Thinking outside the box of the creative individual.* New York, NY: Springer.

Glăveanu, V. P. (2014b). *Thinking through creativity and culture: Toward an integrated model.* New Brunswick, NJ: Transaction Publishers.

Glăveanu, V. P. (2014c). Revisiting the "art bias" in lay conceptions of creativity. *Creativity Research Journal*, *26*(1), 11–20.

Glăveanu, V. P., et al. (2019). Advancing creativity theory and research: A sociocultural manifesto. *Journal of Creative Behaviour*. Retrieved from: https://doi.org/10.1002/jocb.395

Glăveanu, V. P., & Clapp, E. P. (2018). Distributed and participatory creativity as a form of cultural empowerment: The role of alterity, difference, and collaboration. In A. U. Branco & M. C. Lopes-de-Oliveira (Eds.), *Alterity, values, and socialization: Human development within educational contexts* (pp. 51–63). Cham, Switzerland: Springer.

Goldberg, A., & Zunon, E. (2022). *Bottle tops: The art of El Anatsui.* New York: Lee & Low Books.

Great Schools Partnership. (2014, May 14). Competency-based learning. *The glossary of education reform*. Retrieved from: https://www.edglossary.org/competency-based-learning/

Gruber, H. E. (1981). *Darwin on man*. Chicago: University of Chicago Press.

Gruber, H. E., & Davis, S. N. (1988). Inching our way up Mount Olympus: The evolving systems approach to creative thinking. In R. J. Sternberg (Ed.), *The nature of creativity: Contemporary psychological perspectives* (pp. 243–270). Cambridge, UK: Cambridge University Press.

Gruber, H. E., & Wallace, D. B. (1999). The case study method and evolving systems approach for understanding unique creative people at work. In R. J. Sternberg (Ed.), *Handbook of creativity* (pp. 93–115). Cambridge, UK: Cambridge University Press.

Hanchett Hanson, M. (2015). *Worldmaking: Psychology and the ideology of creativity*. London, UK: Palgrave Macmillan.

Hanchett Hanson, M., & Clapp, E. P. (2020). Participatory creativity (encyclopedia entry). In M. Runco (Ed.), *Encyclopedia of creativity* (pp. 300–303). San Diego, CA: Academic Press.

Hattie, J. (2023). *Visible learning: The sequel*. New York: Routledge.

Hutchins, E. (1995). *Cognition in the wild*. Cambridge, MA: The MIT Press.

Jenkins, H., Purushotma, R., Weigel, M., Clinton, K., & Robison, A. J., (2009). *Confronting the challenges of participatory culture: Media education for the 21st Century*. Cambridge, MA: MIT Press.

Kaufman, J. C., & Beghetto, R. A. (2009). Beyond big and little: The four c model of creativity. *Review of General Psychology*, *13*(1), 1–12.

Khan, H. (2012). *Golden domes and silver lanterns. A Muslim book of colors*. San Francisco, CA: Chronicle Books.

Krechevsky, M., Mardell, B., Rivard, M., & Wilson, D. (2013) *Visible learners: Promoting Reggio-inspired approaches in all schools*. San Francisco, CA: Jossey: Bass.

Latour, B. (2005). *Reassembling the social: An introduction to actor-network-theory*. Oxford, UK: Oxford University Press.

Lê, M., & Santat, D. (2018). *Drawn together*. New York: Disney-Hyperion.

Nagel, T. (1986). *The view from nowhere*. New York: Oxford University Press.

Owen, H. (n.d.). *A brief user's guide to open space technology*. Retrieved from: https://openspaceworld.org/wp2/hho/papers/brief-users-guide-open-space-technology/

Pereira, J. L. (2023, May 9). Tracing stories of innovation: A human-centered approach to computer science (conference presentation). *21st Century Learning Conference*. Retrieved from: https://www.21clconf.org/presentations/tracing-stories-of-ideas-a-human-centered-approach-to-computer-science/

Perkins, D. N., Jay, E., & Tishman, S. (1993). Beyond abilities: A dispositional theory of thinking. *Merrill-Palmer Quarterly, 39*(1), 1–21.

Project Zero/Cultures of Thinking. (n.d.). *Looking at Students' Thinking (LAST) Protocol*. Retrieved from: https://pz.harvard.edu/sites/default/files/LAST%2Bprotocol_New.pdf

Ricci, J. L. (2020). The SEED framework for cultivating creativity (encyclopedia entry). In M. A. Peters & R. Heraud (Eds.), *Encyclopedia of educational innovation*. Springer Nature Singapore Pte Ltd. Retrieved from: https://doi.org/10.1007/978-981-13-2262-4_106-1

Ritchhart, R. (2015). *Cultures of thinking: The 8 forces we must master to transform our schools*. San Francisco, CA: Jossey Bass.

Ritchhart, R., & Church, M. (2020). *The power of making thinking visible: Practices to engage and empower all learners*. San Francisco, CA: Jossey Bass.

Rodriguez, B. (2017). *The power of creative constraints (TED talk)*. Retrieved from https://ed.ted.com/lessons/the-power-of-creative-constraints-brandon-rodriguez

Saeed, A. (2018). *Amal unbound: A novel*. New York: Nancy Paulsen Books.

Sawyer, K., & DeZutter, S. (2009). Distributed creativity: How collective creations emerge from collaboration. *Psychology of Aesthetics, Creativity, and the Arts, 3*(2), 81–92.

Sawyer, R. K. (2007). *Group genius: The creative power of collaboration*. New York, NY: Basic Books.

Sawyer, R. K. (2010). Individual and group creativity. In J. C. Kaufman & R. J. Sternberg (Eds.), *The Cambridge handbook of creativity* (pp. 366–381). Cambridge, UK: Cambridge University Press.

Sawyer, R. K. (Ed.). (2011). *Structure and improvisation in creative teaching*. Cambridge, UK: Cambridge University Press.

Sawyer, R. K. (2012). *Explaining creativity: The science of human innovation*. Oxford, UK: Oxford University Press.

Senge, P. M. (1990). *The fifth discipline: The art and practice of the learning organization*. New York: Doubleday.

Shetterly, M. L. (2016). *Hidden figures: The untold true story of four African-American women who helped launch our nation into space.* New York: Harper.

Simonton, D. K. (1999). *Origins of genius: Darwinian perspectives on creativity.* Oxford, UK: Oxford University Press.

Simonton, D. K. (2004). *Creativity and science.* New York: Cambridge University Press.

Stager, G., & Martinez, S. L. (2013). *Invent to learn.* Torrance, CA: Constructing Modern Knowledge Press.

Sweeney, L. B. (2012). Learning to connect the dots: Developing children's systems literacy, *Solutions, 5*(3), 55–62.

Tishman, S. (2017). *Slow looking: The art and practice of learning through observation.* New York: Routledge.

Torrance, P. E. (2018). *Torrance tests of creative thinking: Interpretive manual.* Bensenville, IL: Scholastic Testing Services. Retrieved from: https://www.ststesting.com/gift/TTCT_InterpMOD.2018.pdf

Tromp, C. (in press). *The power of creative constraints.* New York: Oxford University Press.

Vygotsky, L. S. (1978). *Mind in society: The development of higher psychological processes.* Cambridge, MA: Harvard University Press.

Wallace, D. B., & Gruber, H. E. (Eds.). (1989). *Creative people at work.* Oxford, UK: Oxford University Press.

Wardrip, P., Evancho, J., & McNamara, A. (2018). Identifying what matters. *Phi Delta Kappan, 99*(6), 60–63.

Winner, E. (1991). *Arts PROPEL: An introductory handbook.* Educational Testing Service and Presidents and Fellows of Harvard College.

For Product Safety Concerns and Information please contact our
EU representative GPSR@taylorandfrancis.com Taylor & Francis
Verlag GmbH, Kaufingerstraße 24, 80331 München, Germany